True Worship

Donald Werner
3/17/2022

Copyright

Also, please note; God sacred name, YHVH (sometimes pronounced, Yahoveh, Jehoveh, or Yahweh) was in the original Hebrew Bible more than 2000 times. However, the Bible translators, for centuries, have removed God's sacred name from the Bible and replaced it with the phrase 'the LORD'. In the verses which I have included in this book, I have restored God's sacred name YHVH where the translator had substituted 'the LORD'. I did that for clarity and understanding.

Contents

THE PREFACE

I attended a major Protestant seminary, but in my senior year I found that it was impossible reconcile Jesus' words with Christian Church doctrines, so I had to choose between Jesus and the Church. I chose to follow Jesus and dropped out of the seminary. In keeping with Jesus' words, I made him my only teacher. So, I set the rest of the New Testament aside and focused on Jesus' words alone. After focusing on Jesus' words, I had to separated myself from the Christian Church to follow Jesus. After 70 years in the Christian Church, I now understand how its worship dishonors both Jesus and God. I will explain all of that and more in this book.

Isaiah 66:22-23, **"For as the new heavens and the new earth which I will make shall remain before Me,"** says YHVH, **"So shall your descendants and your name remain. 23 And it shall come to pass that from one New Moon to another, And from one Sabbath to another, All flesh shall come to worship before Me,"** says YHVH.

YHVH God is planning on a future eternal kingdom (Isaiah 66:22-23), and according to (John 4:23), the Father is now seeking true worshipers who will worship Him in 'truth and spirit' - now and in His future kingdom. However, Christians do not worship in 'truth and spirit'.

Since the Father only wants true worshiper for His kingdom, we need to learn what that means and how to be a true worshiper of God. Who did Jesus say we should worship? How important is it that we worship God? When are we to worship? What causes people's worship to be false worship, or in vain? Who are we to worship? What is wrong with Christian worship? What does it mean to worship the 'beast' or his 'image'? These questions and more will be answered in this book.

So, put your seat belt on, lower your defenses by setting aside manmade creeds and church doctrines, and open your mind to Jesus' words, and then hang on for a ride that will change your life now, as well as your eternal life.

End

THE INTRODUCTION

A major theme of the Bible, and perhaps the greatest theme is that of worship. We are commanded many times in the Scriptures to worship God, give glory to God and praise God. Those commands to worship are so frequent that it's clear that it's reason and purpose which we were created. And if we are redeemed, it's the reason that we are redeemed. We were created by God to glorify God, to worship God and praise God.

Psalm 95:6, **"Oh come, let us worship and bow down; let us kneel before YHVH, our Maker!"** Isaiah 43:7, **"Everyone who is called by My name, Whom I have created for My glory; I have formed him, yes, I have made him."** Isaiah 43:21, **"This people I have formed for Myself; They shall declare My praise".**

To be redeemed we are required to worship YHVH God now, and we will be doing it every Sabbath for all eternity. God seeks true worshipers for His future kingdom. Those who are not true worshipers are not fit for God's kingdom. All truly saved people are true worshipers and all true worshipers will be redeemed. So, since God will save all true worshipers, being a true worshiper is synonymous with salvation.

As we study what it means to truly worship God in this book, we will pay particular attention to Jesus' words. Why? According to Deuteronomy 18:18-19, Acts 3:22, 7:37, John 12:49 and John 14:10, Jesus spoke YHVH God's words with YHVH God's authority. And there is no greater authority. Jesus also tells us that he is to be our only teacher. Because of the authority by which Jesus spoke, this study will focus on Jesus' words. We read in John 12:48-50 that Jesus will be our judge, he will judge us according to he we kept his words, and he said his words are not his, but they are from YHVH God.

Since Jesus spoke YHVH's words with YHVH's authority so we better take heed to Jesus' words. Jesus said in Matthew 23:10 (NKJV), **"And do not be called teachers; for One is your Teacher, the Christ"..** Since Jesus is to be our only teacher, we can trust that he will teach all we need to know about salvation, and that includes all we need to know about how to be a true worshiper.

Among God's final commands in the Scriptures to mankind was the command to; '**Worship God**' (Revelation 14:7) and then He commanded for His people to 'come out' of the religious system that worships the 'beast' and the 'image of the beast', and that religious system is known as Babylon

(Revelation 18:4). And Babylon, as we will learn is the fallen Christian Church which God calls us out of.

Donald Werner, dxwerne@yahoo.com

Chapter 1 – TRUE WORSHIP VS. FALSE WORSHIP

WHO ARE WE TO WORSHIP?

Perhaps the most important issue about true worship is that our worship is directed to the correct being. If we worship someone other than the true God, that is referred to as idolatry, and according, to Jesus, no idolater will be allowed into God's kingdom (Revelation 21:15, 22:8). True worship is the key to getting into God's kingdom and to do that we need to know the correct object of worship, that is essential to true worship.

We can listen to Jesus about who to worship, but some may ask, who is Jesus that we should listen to Him? We read in Deuteronomy 18 that YHVH God said that in the future He would anoint a prophet (Christ or Messiah), who like Moses would to speak YHVH's words with His authority. Then we read in Acts 3:22 that Peter says that Jesus is that Anointed Prophet. We read in Acts 7:37 that Stephen also says Jesus is that Anointed Prophets. And we read in John's Revelation 22:8-9 where John also identifies Jesus as that Prophets. Then Jesus himself tells us that he spoke YHVH's words with YHVH's authority (John 12:49, 14:10). So if we believe the Scriptures, we have to believe that Jesus spoke YHVH's word with His authority, so we must listen to Jesus as though it is YHVH speaking. And, indeed, Jesus' words in the New Testament are all compatible with YHVH's words in the Old Testament. So Jesus' words are the 'gold standard' by which all other words and teachings must agree with.

John 12:48-50, **"He who rejects Me, and does not receive My words, has that which judges him—the word that I have spoken will judge him in the last day. 49 For I have not spoken on My own authority; but the Father who sent Me gave Me a command, what I should say and what I should speak. 50 And I know that His command is everlasting life. Therefore, whatever I speak, just as the Father has told Me, so I speak."** This is why Jesus said that he is to be our only teacher, others may persuade us to not fully obey all that Jesus commanded. For salvation, Jesus must be our absolute authority, not Paul, Peter, James, John, Jude nor any other New Testament writer. All other New Testament writers must agree 100% with what Jesus said, or their writings must be discarded.

So, who did Jesus tell us to worship? Matthew 4:10 and Luke 4:8, **" Jesus answered, "It is written: 'Worship the LORD your God and serve him only.'"** If we examine this verse in the Old Testament (Deuteronomy 6:13) we will see that **'the LORD'** is God's sacred name, YHVH, or Yahoveh, or Jehoveh, or Yahweh. Different people use different pronunciations for the Hebrew name, YHVH. So what Jesus really said was, **"It is written: 'Worship YHVH your God and serve him only.'"**

Here is a Heavenly scene, Jesus and YHVH are both in heaven, and the question is; who is it that 'every creature' in heaven worship? Revelation 5:13-14, **"And every creature which is in heaven and on the earth and under the earth and such as are in the sea, and all that are in them, I heard saying: "Blessing and honor and glory and power Be to Him who sits on the throne** *(YHVH)*, **And to the Lamb** *(Jesus)*, **forever and ever!"**
14 Then the four living creatures said, "Amen!" And the twenty-four elders fell down and worshiped Him *(YHVH)* **who lives forever and ever."**

In verse 13 **"blessing and honor and glory and power"** went to Jesus and YHVH, but then in verse 14 they don't worship Jesus (the Lamb), but they only worship **'Him who lives forever and ever'**. A number of verses in the Book of the Revelation, and through the Scriptures we find the use of the phrases **"Him who created all thing'** and **"Him who sits on the throne"** and **'Him who lives forever"** to identify YHVH God. Even though Jesus was present in heaven, they only worshiped YHVH God. That's whom Jesus told us to worship alone, Matthew 4:10 and Luke 4:8.

What did Jesus tell us about who it is that we are to worship? Jesus pointed to the same object of worship that the Old Testament Prophets did, and that is the same object of worship that YHVH tells us to worship. In Matthew 4:10 we read, **"Then Jesus said to him, "Away with you, Satan! For it is written, 'You shall worship YHVH your God, and Him only you shall serve' "**. Jesus told us to worship and serve YHVH God alone. So here, Jesus clearly tells us who the only object of our worship is to be, and that is YHVH God and YHVH God alone.

In Revelation 14:1 we read that all who are (will be) redeemed from the earth have the Father's name, YHVH, written on (or in) their foreheads. And in Revelation 22:8-9 Jesus was the angel of God (the Greek word 'angel' means 'messenger') who tell John to not worship him, but instead to worship God. We know it was Jesus who was speaking to John because the description of the speaker in 22:9 only fits Jesus. Jesus message to us is to worship YHVH God alone, the one who is also our 'Father'.

The Christian Church will tell us that God's First Commandment is ; **'You shall have no other gods before me'**. But unfortunately that is incomplete because it is taken out of context. To understand that context of that Commandment we have to also read the verse before it. When reading YHVH's First Commandment, written in stone with His own finger, we need to read Exodus 20 verses 2 and 3. Then we will understand who it is that is speaking the Commandments, we also learn God's name, and who it is that we are to worship. This is God's First Commandment, Exodus 20:2-3, **"I am YHVH your God who brought you out of the land of Egypt out of the house of bondage, you shall have no other gods before me"**. When both verses are read together, it is clear that we are to worship YHVH God alone, just as Jesus said in Matthew 4:10.

In Zechariah, another end-time apocalyptic book, we read that God's final test for mankind will have to do with who is their God. Zechariah 13:8-9,"**And it shall come to pass in all the land," Says YHVH, "That two-thirds in it shall be cut off and die, but one-third shall be left in it: 9 I will bring the one-third through the fire, will refine them as silver is refined, And test them as gold is tested. They will call on My name, And I will answer them. I will say, 'This is My people'; And each one will say, 'YHVH is my God.'"** This is perhaps that last test for mankind, because it happens during the plague, bowls, or judgments when two-thirds of the earth is destroyed. The one third that is left is subjected to a fiery test of pain, suffer, grief, sorrow, hunger, etc. In the midst of that suffering, whoever believes in a god will cry out to their god for relief from their suffering. Only those who cry out to YHVH will be identified by YHVH God as His people and they will be saved. All the others cried out to some other god and were not redeemed. Joel 2:32, **"And it shall come to pass that whoever calls on the name of YHVH shall be saved..."**

Clearly, Old Testament and New Testament Scripture all tell us to worship YHVH God alone. There is no indication that anyone else in the Scriptures should be worshiped. So who is YHVH God? According to 1Chronicles 29:10, Isaiah 63:16, Isaiah 68:4, Malachi 1:6 and other verses, YHVH God is our Father. Jesus said YHVH is the one and only true God (Mark 12:29) whom we are to worship alone (Matthew 4:10, Luke 4:8) and that YHVH is one. In John 17:3 Jesus prayed to the Father that everyone would know that YHVH is the only true God and that Jesus, himself, was His Messiah, or Christ – and Jesus said salvation depends on us knowing that.

JESUS CLEARLY STATED THAT THERE IS NO TRINITY

Here Jesus offers irrefutable proof that there is no Trinity.

Mark 12:28-29, **"Then one of the scribes came, and having heard them reasoning together, perceiving that He had answered them well, asked Him, "Which is the first** *(chief or greatest)* **commandment of all?"**
29 Jesus answered him, "The first *(chief or greatest)* **of all the commandments is: 'Hear, O Israel, the YHVH God, YHVH is one."**

32 "So the scribe said to Him *(Jesus),* **"Well said, Teacher. You have spoken the truth, for there is one God, and there is no other but He. 33 And to love Him** *(YHVH)* **with all the heart, with all the**

understanding, with all the soul, and with all the strength, and to love one's neighbor as oneself, is more than all the whole burnt offerings and sacrifices."

34 Now when Jesus saw that he answered wisely, He said to him, "You are not far from the kingdom of God."

The scribe said there is one God and only one God, and Jesus said he answered **'wisely'** and said he was **"not far from the kingdom of God"**.

Jesus praying to our Father (YHVH) said, **"And this is eternal life, that they may know You, the only true God, and Jesus Christ whom, You have sent"** (John 17:3 NKJV). Eternal life depends on us knowing that YHVH is **"the only true God"**. And therefore the worship of anyone other than YHVH is idolatry. And Jesus said no idolater will enter the kingdom of heaven, but will be burned with a consuming fire (Revelation 21:8, 22:15).

Jesus quoted the Old Testament in Mark 12:29, where he is asked what is the most important commandment of God, he answered, **"The most important one," answered Jesus, "is this: 'Hear, O Israel: YHVH our God, YHVH is one."** The most important commandment, according to Jesus, is the acknowledgement that there is one God and God is one and God's name is YHVH. If this is the greatest commandment, then the greatest sin is the violation of this commandment, which is idolatry. Jesus said in the Book of the Revelation, that idolaters will not enter the kingdom of God.

YHVH CLEARLY STATES THAT THERE IS NO TRINITY

YHVH God etched in stone with His own fingers the Ten Commandments, the first, and most important commandments is found in Exodus 20:2-3, **"I am YHVH your God, who brought you out of the land of Egypt, out of the house of bondage you shall have no other gods before Me."** This commandment leaves no room of Jesus being God or for God being a Trinity. And 'YHVH God' is not a trinity, YHVH is God and YHVH is our Father; 1Chronicles 29:10, **"Therefore David blessed YHVH before all the assembly; and David said: "Blessed are You, YHVH God of Israel, our Father, forever and ever."**

Isaiah 63:16, **"Doubtless You are our Father, though Abraham was ignorant of us, And Israel does not acknowledge us. You, O YHVH, are our Father; Our Redeemer from Everlasting is Your name."**

Isaiah 64:8, **"But now, O YHVH, You are our Father; We are the clay, and You our potter; And all we are the work of Your hand."**

Malachi 1:6, **"A son honors his father, and a servant his master. If then I am the Father, Where is My honor? And if I am a Master, Where**

is My reverence? Says YHVH of hosts to you priests who despise My name. Yet you say, 'In what way have we despised Your name?'

YHVH is our Father, and He is the only true God, and He is one. YHVH is the same Being that Jesus said was his 'Father and God' (John 20:17). In John 14:28, Jesus said he was not co-equal to his Father, for his Father was greater than he was.

YHVH, our God and Father is not the same "Father" that is part of the Trinity, for YHVH God will have nothing to do with the Trinity, for He said that He will not share His glory, honor, praise or worship with another. He is a jealous God and a consuming fire and unless we honor, praise, and worship Him alone as God, we will be destroyed by that consuming fire.

THERE IS NO EVIDENCE FOR THE TRINITY IN THE BIBLE

Who else in the Scriptures invalidates the idea of a triune god, or a Trinity by acknowledging that YHVH God is one? YHVH God is one and only one according to: YHVH (Exodus 20:2-3), according to Jesus (Matthew 4:10, 6:9, Mark 12:29, Luke 4:8, John 17:3), according to Moses (Deuteronomy 4:35, 6:4), according to the Prophet Isaiah (Isaiah 44:6, Isaiah 45:6, 37:20 45:18.), according to the Prophet Samuel (1Samuel 2:2), according to King Hezekiah (2 Kings 19:15), according to King David (1 Chronicles 17:20, Psalm 18:31) according to King Solomon (1King 8:23), according to the Prophet Nehemiah (Nehemiah 9:6-7), according to Asaph (Psalm 83:18), according to Hannah (1Samuel 2:2), according to the Prophet Jeremiah, (Jeremiah 22:9), according to the Prophet Hosea (Hosea 13:4), according to the Prophet Joel (Joel 2:27), according to the Prophet Zechariah (Zechariah 14:9), according to the Prophet Malachi (Malachi 2:10), according to Paul (Ephesians 4:6, 1Timothy 2:5), according to James (James 2:19), according to Peter (2Peter 1:2) and according to Jude (Jude 1:25). No writer in the Old or New Testament acknowledges, defines or mentions a triune god.

Never is Jesus referred to as God, but he tells us that he has a God and a Father (John 20:17). Even those who know that there is no Trinity will acknowledge that there is a Father, and there is a Son and there is a holy spirit, but they are not three gods and Scriptures never defines them as three gods, or a trinity. There are no gods, or Gods who are co-equal or co-eternal to our Father, YHVH. In John 14:28 Jesus said he is not co-equal with the Father, why can't Christians hear him? While there are many gods in the Bible (the word 'god' simply means 'great one'), but there is only one Almighty God, and that is our Father, YHVH God.

Worshiping the Trinity, or worshiping Jesus or Mary, is contrary to what Jesus commanded and it's contrary to what YHVH commanded. And the rejection of Jesus' command or YHVH's commands dishonors Jesus and YHVH, and it is idolatry. Somehow Christians figure that they are honoring Jesus and earning salvation by worshiping Jesus, but they are mistaken, because just the opposite is true. Christians dishonor Jesus and YHVH by the rejection of their commandments to worship YHVH alone. When we reject YHVH's or Jesus' commands, it's because we were told it is OK to do that, by some other authority that we have allowed to trump over YHVH's words and Jesus' words.

We all have been taught in our Christian training that Jesus is God. We have been told that he is the second person in the Trinity. However, none of that is not is found in the Scriptures, the Scriptures do not support Jesus being God, nor does it support the idea that there is a Trinity – the Scriptures teach just the opposite. Jesus clearly and succinctly told us that YHVH is the only true God (Mark 12:28-29, John 17:3), and we are to worship YHVH alone (Matthew 4:10), yet Christians have been deceived into believing that Jesus is God and that they must worship him as God to be saved. And most Christians are easy to deceive because they don't read or study the Scriptures for themselves.

When people are deceived into believing that Jesus is God, and they read Matthew 4:10, "**... For it is written, 'You shall worship the Lord your God, and Him only you shall serve'**". They automatically assume that 'the LORD' is Jesus or the Trinity. Or when they read in Act 2:21, **"And everyone who calls on the name of the Lord will be saved.'** We automatically assume 'the LORD' is Jesus. But we know that these verses are quotes from the Old Testament and where we read, '**the LORD'**, the original verse said, '**YHVH'**. So what they really say is, "**... For it is written, 'You shall worship YHVH your God, and Him only you shall serve'** ". And, "**And everyone who calls on the name of YHVH will be saved.'** Thus identifying YHVH as the one true God.

For a number reasons, God's name "YHVH" was stripped out of the Bible and replaced with the phrase 'the LORD'. While the intentions were to protect YHVH's name from being misused, however, the substitution added some confusion to the text for to those who don't have access to the Hebrew Scriptures. So I restored 'YHVH' name the verses which I quote.

Some Christians have read that they are to worship YHVH alone, so they make the mistake of claiming that Jesus must be YHVH. Yet, the Scriptures clearly tell us that Jesus is not YHVH God, YHVH God is his Father and our Father and the Father of Israel His first born son (Exodus 4:22). The fact that Jesus said, 'I and the Father are one' doesn't mean they are literally the same being. They are one in spirit and one thought, in the same manner that a married couple is one. Jesus also prayed that he and his followers would be one. Jesus and the Father are one in that Jesus was anointed by the Father to speak His words with His authority; so, when Jesus spoke it was the Father speaking through Him. In that respect they are one.

True Worship

YHVH and Jesus are clearly two completely distinct individuals (John 14:1, 14:28, 17:3, 20:17), but their beliefs, focus and their goals are one. Jesus is not YHVH God and YHVH God is not Jesus, YHVH God is not the Trinity and the Trinity is not YHVH God. YHVH God is not part of the Trinity. YHVH said that He alone is God and there are no others. YHVH God, Our Father, cannot be part of a Trinity because He is a jealous God and He will not share His glory, praise, or worship with another. Isaiah 42:8, **"I am YHVH, that is My name; and My glory I will not give to another, nor My praise to carved images."** Exodus 34:14, YHVH said, **"... you shall worship no other god, for YHVH, whose name is Jealous, is a jealous God".** Being a "Jealous God" means that YHVH is God alone and He will allow no other god to steal or to share in His glory, praise or worship, nor will He share the credit for His creation, or redemption. Isaiah 44:2, **"Thus says YHVH, the King of Israel, And his Redeemer, YHVH of hosts: 'I am the First and I am the Last; Besides Me there is no god."** That is perfectly clear, even with the understanding of a child. Only those who are willfully ignorant, deceived, or drunk on the wine of Babylon, could be confused by the contents of that verse – or perhaps they will not accept the plain meaning of it so that they can hang on to the doctrine of man, the doctrine of the Trinity.

The Scriptures tell us that Jesus is not God and he says that he has a God and a Father who had begotten him; John 20:17, **"Jesus said to her, "Do not cling to Me, for I have not yet ascended to My Father; but go to My brethren and say to them, 'I am ascending to My Father and your Father, and to My God and your God.'"** In John 14:1 Jesus said, **"Let not your heart be troubled; you believe in God, believe also in me."** John 14:28, **"...I am going to the Father, for the Father is greater than I."**

Matthew 19:16-17, **"Now behold, one came and said to Him, "Good Teacher, what good thing shall I do that I may have eternal life?"**
17 **So He** (Jesus) **said to him, "Why do you call Me good? No one is good but One, that is,** (YHVH) **God. But if you want to enter into life, keep the commandments."** The Greek word for 'good' here means 'perfect'. So, Jesus is saying, I'm not perfect, but YHVH God is perfect, and therefore I'm not YHVH God.

WAS JESUS WORSHIPED?

And yes, I know that there are some translations of the Bible that say Jesus was worshiped, but that is certainly not the case. The Greek word translated 'worship', could also be translated as to 'kneel before', 'bow before', 'prostrate before' or to show reverence. These acts of reverence were done to one who is an important person, king, miracle worker, true prophet, highly respected rabbi or highly respected teacher. And Jesus could fit all of those 'important persons' categories without even being considered to be God and he was highly reverenced. Instead of saying 'worship, some translations say, 'people bowed before him' or 'knelt before him'. In the Old Testament we read that 'Jacob bowed before Pharaoh, and Joseph's brother bowed before Joseph. A translator could have translated those verses as saying the 'Jacob worshiped the Pharaoh', or that 'Joseph's brothers worship Joseph'. But that didn't make sense because of the character of the people involved so they translated that word as 'bowed'. If the translators believe that Jesus is God, they are likely to translate the word as 'worship'. If the translators weren't pre-disposed to believe that Jesus was God, they may use the word 'bow'. Using the word 'worship' doesn't make Jesus into God, it reflects the translator's belief.

Never did people believe that Jesus was Almighty God in the flesh. If people truly believed that Jesus was God, they would not have addressed him as 'good teacher' or 'rabbi', nor would have they treated his as they did, in such a cavalier way, and he was never worshiped as God, because nobody believed he was Almighty God, although they bowed before him and reverenced him as a great prophet, inspired teacher and miracle worker. They all knew that YHVH alone was the one true God.

There were a number of people, angels and beings in the Scriptures that are referred to as a 'god'. But the word 'god' simply means 'great one'. However, there is only one that is referred to as 'Almighty God'.

Here are nine different translations of Matthew 14:33;

CJB – "The men in the boat **fell down before** him ..."
CEV- "The men in the boat **worshiped** Jesus ..."
DARBY – "But those in the ship came and **did homage** to him ..."
DRA – "And they that were in the boat came and **adored him**, ..."
NEC – "Those in the boat **fell to their knees** in worship..."
NKJV – "Then those who were in the boat **worshiped him**"
TLB – "The others sat there, **awestruck**..."
NOG – "The men in the boat **bowed down in front of Yeshua...**"
WE – "Then the men in the boat **bowed down in front of Jesus...**"

The translators have much latitude as to which word, or phrase, to use in these verses. The same Greek word may be translated a number of ways. However, they word used by the translators will reflect the theological bent of the translator. When translator uses the word 'worship' it is because he/she believes that Jesus is God, and the reader also then assumes that Jesus is God.

Christian translators will generally use the word 'worship' because they have the presumption that Jesus is God. So, we can't assume Jesus is God just because the text says they 'worshiped' him, it could correctly say that they bowed before him, as they did for highly respected people, such as prophets and great rabbis.

JESUS SAID, DON'T WORSHIP ME, WORSHIP YHVH GOD

Jesus said in Matthew 4:10 that we are serve and worship YHVH God alone. In the revelation given to John he tried to worship the glorified Jesus in Revelation 22:8-9 and Jesus said to John, 'don't worship me, worship God'. We know that it was Jesus speaking those words because Revelation 22:9 defines who is was that said, 'don't worship me, worship God'. Revelation 22:9, **"But he said to me, "Don't do that! I am a fellow servant with you and with your fellow prophets and with all who keep the words of this scroll. Worship God!"** That description spoken to John in vs. 9 can only be of Jesus, because that description doesn't work to describe angels, for angels are not 'fellow prophets' of John, although Jesus was. In Matthew 15:37, and other verses, Jesus identified himself as a prophet. While vs. 8 does say it was an 'angel' who spoke these words, however, the word 'angel' in the Greek word simply means 'messenger'. Jesus, according to Revelation 1:1 was God's 'messenger' (i.e. angel) to show John all things. It was Jesus, God's messenger, who told John to not worship him, but instead to "worship God".

In Matthew 2:2-11, the translator of this verse, and a few other versions, said the Magi came to worship Jesus. The Magi did not come to "worship" a baby God, they came to show reverence to a new born "king of the Jews". They came to 'show reverence' or to 'bow' before the new born king as it was custom to bow before a king. To 'show reverence' or to 'bow' is the same Greek word that is sometimes translated as 'worship'. Some other translations say, 'pay homage', 'knelt', 'honored' or 'bowed'. The word 'worship' would only be used by translators who believe in the 'Trinity'. But the Scriptures tell us that Jesus was God's anointed messiah, he was not Almighty God. Not one verse in the Bible says that Jesus is God, but there are many claims that he was an anointed prophet and a separate being from YHVH God.

Regardless of what a few misguided individual may say, Jesus is not YHVH God. According to King David (1Chronicles 29:10) and the Prophet Isaiah (Isaiah 63:16, 64:8), the Prophet Malachi (Malachi 1:16) and other verses, YHVH is Our Father, because He created us. It was YHVH whom anointed Jesus as His messiah (Deuteronomy 18:18-19, Acts 3:22, and Acts 7:37). Jesus said YHVH was his God and his Father, as well as our God and our Father (John 20:17), and Jesus said that YHVH was the only true God, (John 17:3) and he, himself, was YHVH's anointed Prophet (Messiah or Christ). Jesus prayed to YHVH God, and he worshiped YHVH God.

Isaiah 42:8, **"I am YHVH, that is My name; And My glory I will not give to another, nor My praise to carved images."**

It was to our Father that Jesus prayed, and it is to our Father that Jesus told us to pray to (Matthew 6). Jesus said Our Father was also his God (John 20:17, Revelation 3:2, 12) and our God. Jesus, using the pronoun 'we', said that he was among the Jews who worshiped our Father (John 4:22-23), and that's whom Jesus told us to worship (Matthew 4:10). Jesus told us to go to our Father for forgiveness (Matthew 6:15), just as he sought forgiveness from the Father for those who crucified him (Luke 23:34). It's YHVH's laws that we violate when we sin, so, it's His forgiveness that we need, so don't apologize to Jesus.

In Matthew 4:10 and Luke 4:8 Jesus said, "**... For it is written, 'You shall worship YHVH your God, and Him only you shall serve' "**. Jesus told us 'worship' and 'serve' YHVH our God alone. In the next chapter we will see what it means to worship.

WE ARE TO WORSHIP AND SERVE YHVH ALONE

The next chapter is devoted to what it means to worship God but, what does it means to 'serve' God? One of the definitions for the Hebrew and Greek word "serve" means; "to render religious service or homage." That means that all we do in our religious services: praying light candles, bowing, singing, chanting, and (or) giving sacrifice must all be directed to YHVH God, and not Jesus, not Mary, nor the Trinity, nor any saint. And I know, that's just the opposite of what we see and hear in our Christian Churches today, but that's what the YHVH and Jesus both commanded. That's what the Jews do in their synagogues, and Jesus said 'salvation is of the Jews' (John 4:22).

All prayers must be addressed to YHVH, all forgiveness must be sought from YHVH, and all worship related activities must be directed towards YHVH God alone. That's what Jesus commands and he freely acknowledged many times that he is not God, and he tells us to worship and serve YHVH God alone. Yet those in the Christian Church are deceived into worshiping Jesus as God. In reality they are not really worship of Jesus is in vain, for he will not accept their worship.

People are deceived into believing that Jesus is God, so they worship him and pray to him thinking that somehow they are honoring him. But, just the opposite is true. Jesus told us that he is not God and we are to worship YHVH alone. So, when people worship Jesus, or the Trinity, they are disobeying Jesus' command (Matthew 4:10, Luke 4:8), and disobeying YHVH's commands (Exodus 20:2-3) – and to disobey their commands is to dishonor them. Thus when someone worships Jesus, or the Trinity, they are actually dishonoring Jesus and dishonoring YHVH God by rejecting what they have commanded. And instead of worshiping YHVH, they are obeying the doctrines of a religious organization, which gives us the deceptive messages of the 'beast'.

Psalm 96:9, "**Oh, worship YHVH in the beauty of holiness! Tremble before Him, all the earth.**"

True Worship

End

Chapter 2 –WORSHIP

WORSHIP IS COMMANDED BY THE EVERLASTING GOSPEL

The Book of the Revelation is God's last message to mankind, we read what is perhaps God's last command to mankind is found in Revelation 22:9, and we also see in Revelation 14:7, which command is to 'Worship YHVH God'. Revelation 14:7 (NKJV), "**saying with a loud voice, "<u>Fear God</u> and <u>give glory to Him</u>, for the hour of His judgment has come; and <u>worship Him</u> who made heaven and earth, the sea and springs of water.**" That is the Everlasting Gospel.

The last command of the Everlasting Gospel is, "**<u>worship Him</u> who made heaven and earth, the sea and springs of water.**" If we go to the Forth Commandments (Exodus 20:11) to see who it was that "**made the heaven and earth, the sea and the springs of water**", we will see that it was YHVH God. So, it's clear that the "God" spoken about in this everlasting Gospel is YHVH God, also known as our 'Father' (Isaiah 63:16, 64:8, 2Chronicles 29:10, Malachi 1:6). Our Father's name, 'YHVH', is the same name that all of the redeemed (the 144,000 in verse Revelation 14:1) had written 'in' or 'on' their foreheads. The Everlasting Gospel is really telling us to fear YHVH God, glorify YHVH God and worship YHVH God.

WORSHIP, WHAT IS IT?

The word 'worship' is a common word in the Bible, it appears nearly 200 times. The word 'worship' appears 22 times in the Book of the Revelation alone, that's more than it appears in any other Book of the Bible. God requires that His people are true worshiper of Him, and that doesn't mean that they go to church weekly. Going to a Christian Church service is not true worship, and I will tell you why later.

In the Book of the Revelation, God's last book to mankind, we read His last message to mankind, His last warnings, His last instructions, and His last commands. Worship is the major theme of that Book – YHVH wants to let us know how to worship correctly. And that starts with the correct object of worship.

TWO OBJECTS OF WORSHIP

True Worship

Revelation 14:11, **"And the smoke of their torment ascends forever and ever; and they have no rest day or night, who worship the beast and his image, and whoever receives the mark of his name."** The 'beast' is the devil, Satan, the dragon, and the serpent beast of Genesis. The 'beast's message as given in the Garden of Eden is to 'spurn YHVH's divine authority and thus making 'self' your new god and there will be no eternal consequences for doing that, surely you will not die.' The 'image of the beast' is then any religious organization that reflects the beast's deceptive message by its preaching and (or) teaching. The Christian Church reflects the beast's message when it tells people to 'spurn YHVH's divine authority by rejecting His Old Testament 'law and the Prophets' and to worship a Trinity instead of YHVH, and surely we won't die eternally for doing that. That message mirrors the 'beast' message and that makes the Christian Church into the 'image of the beast' giving out the same lawless message.

In contrast to the 'image of the beast' mirroring the message of the beast, Jesus is the prophet of YHVH who mirrors YHVH's message.

The two choices to worship are; to worship the beast by submitting to the teachings of 'the image of the beast' or to YHVH God by submitting to the teaching s of His anointed Prophet, Jesus.

Now that we understand who the 'beast' is (Satan), and who the 'image of the beast' is (religious institutions), it is very important understand the why and how submissive obedience is worship. It is worship because it is showing great worth to an authority by voluntarily submission to its laws and commands. Our obedience to an authority shows the worth of that authority. If we are willing to obey a certain authority above all other authorities, that is showing greatest worth-ship to that authority – and it honors that authority. If we don't obey an authority, sometimes or all the time, it is showing little worth to that authority – and that dishonors that authority. There is no worship of an authority that we also dishonor. Voluntarily submissive obedience to our greatest authority is an act of worship. If we don't submissively obey an authority we dishonor it and there is no worth-ship.

So, the next question is; to what authority are we going to submit to? There are really only two choices if we consider the "beast and his image" to be one choice and we consider 'YHVH and His Prophet (Jesus)" to be the other choice... The 'image of the Beast' speaks for the Beast, and 'Jesus the prophet' speaks for YHVH.

So, in reality the only two choices; YHVH or the beast. If we obey the teaching of the 'image of the beast' (Churches) we will be worshiping the Beast. The teachings of the Church are to reject YHVH's Old Testament laws and the Prophets, and to worship the Trinity. But, if we obey the teachings of Jesus, we will be worshiping YHVH God. And Jesus' teachings are to keep YHVH's law and the Prophets and to worship YHVH alone. Those are the only two choices and we all must choose. Worship the beast by obeying the commands of the 'image of the beast', or worship YHVH by obeying the commands of Jesus (Prophet of God).

The Book of the Revelation identifies these two different objects of worship; either we are worshiping YHVH God and we will receive the 'seal of YHVH God' or we are worshiping the 'Beast' (or 'his image'), and we will receive the 'mark of the Beast'.

When we submit to YHVH's divine authority, obey Him, it is an act of worship. If we are not submitting to YHVH's divine authority, we are, by default, worshiping the beast. The important lesson we can learn from that is; if we are not true worshiper of 'YHVH God' by our submission to His divine authority, we are worshiping the 'beast'. And unfortunately, the Christian Church tells us that we can spurn YVHV divine authority by ignoring His Old Testament laws, the expression of His authority. If we spurn YHVH's divine authority that means He is not our true God, and we are worshiping a god, other than YHVH God, usually 'self'. To worship any other god is to worship "the beast". Why is what?

And submission obedience is an act of worship, so the question is; who are we obeying Jesus who tells us to keep YHVH's 'law and the Prophets' and worship YHVH alone or are we obeying the 'image of the beast' who tells us don't need to keep YHVH's 'law and the Prophets' and worship the Trinity? That determines who we worship.

The message that we can set aside YHVH's Old Testament 'laws and the Prophets' (spurn YHVH God's divine authority) thereby rejecting YHVH as our true god, originates from the beast (Satan). And that's the same message that Adam and Eve heard in the Garden of Eden. Adam and Eve, or perhaps just Eve, heard it from the serpent beast. He told them that they could spurn YHVH God's authority (His command) and thereby they would be rejecting YHVH as their true God and they could then be their own gods, deciding for themselves what is good and evil, and for doing that there would be no eternal consequences – for the serpent beast assured them that the 'surely would not die'. And that same lawless message is taught and preached in the Christian Church today, thus making the Christian Church the 'image of the beast'. The Church is the 'image of the Beast' because it teaches and preaches the serpent beast's lawless message; telling the people that they can spurn YHVH's authority, express in His Old Testament laws, and to worship a god other than YHVH God alone.

When we talk about 'worshiping the beast' or 'worshiping the image of the beast' the idea is not that people bow down and worship a beast, a statue of the beast, or some other god. The fact is, if we are not submitting to YHVH's

21

True Worship

'laws and the Prophets' we are by default worshiping the 'beast or his image' and not even aware of it. People believe themselves to be good and faithful Christians, and perhaps they are, but by accepting the Christian doctrines they are unwittingly worshiping the beast, or the image of the beast.

So, if we are deceived by the 'image of the beast' (the Christian Church) into spurning YHVH's 'law and the Prophets', and to worship a Trinity, then YHVH is no longer our true god, our worship of Him is in vain.

People who are deceived by the image of the beast believe they are worshiping YHVH God, or Jesus, but since they are rejecting YHVH's commands and Jesus' instructions, and they are actually worshiping the image of the beast by their obedience to the image of the beast's message. These are practicing Christians, but they are unknowingly worshiping the beast or his image – they are not bowing, singing, and chanting to the beast, but by their obedience to the image of the beast they are worshiping it. Voluntarily submissive obedience is the greatest act of worship to God or the beast.

WORSHIP REQUIRES OBEDIENCE

The Greek word and Hebrew word translated as 'worship' really mean to; bow before, kneel or prostrate to do homage, make obeisance, or to show reverence, whether it is done in order to express respect and reverence or to make supplication. The physical position, bowing, kneeling, or prostrated is to be an expression the attitude of the heart. Bowing, kneeling, or prostrating oneself before a being is a sign of humble submission to that being. And if we truly humbly submit ourselves to YHVH's divine authority, we will obey all He commands, including YHVH's Old Testament laws and the Prophet and all spoken by Jesus in the New Testament. That obedience honors YHVH God and demonstrates His great worth to us – and that makes it worth-ship, or worship. Everything else that could be called worship: sacrifice, praise, thanksgiving, reverence, fear, respect, etc., is only acceptable to a God we honor with submissive obedience. Without that submissive obedience, there can be no type of worship. For disobedience dishonors God, and we cannot worship a God that we also dishonor – worship and dishonor are two contrary actions.

WORSHIP BEGINS WITH WORTHSHIP

The Old English word 'worship' is derived for two words; 'worth' and 'ship'. Worship is 'worth-ship', that is exalting some authority as being the greatest worth to us, and that authority of greatest worth is also known as our "supreme authority" and our supreme authority is our true god.

We have many authorities to which we must answer; parents, bosses, police, IRS, teachers, self, doctors, civil authorities, government officials, religious authorities, God, Jesus, etc. All beings express their authority in the laws, commands and rules which they decree. We honor an authority when we obey it, and we dishonor an authority when we disobey it. While we all have many authorities to obey, we all have just one authority which we accept as our supreme authority. Our supreme authority is the one authority that we consider to be of the greatest worth to us and highest authority over us. Obeying our supreme authority, above all other authorities is expressing its great worth to us.

When we receive two opposing or contradicting commands, we have to decide which authority to obey and which to disobey. We will always obey the authority that we consider the greater. So, our supreme authority is the only authority that we will not dishonor with disobedience. So, we can only worship our supreme authority by our submissive obedience. The real question is; who is your supreme authority?

WORSHIP REQUIRES A HUMBLE SUBMISSION

True worship of YHVH God requires that we exalt Him as our supreme authority. However, in order to obey our supreme authority, we must be willing to dishonor all lesser authorities and violate their rules, commands, and laws when they are in conflict with the commands of our supreme authority. We willingly dishonor all lesser authorities by our rejecting, or the setting aside their commands. Then we cannot worship any authority that we have intentionally dishonored, because "worship" and "dishonor" are opposite concepts. So our supreme authority is our true god, and we worship our true god (whoever that is) by submitting to its authority. If we intentionally violate YHVH's commands or laws, we have dishonored Him and then any worship of Him is in vain (Mark 7:7-8). If we worship Jesus, we have violated his command (Matthew 4:10) and our worship of him is in vain. Only true repentance will restore us.

Jesus was anointed by YHVH God to speak with YHVH's words with YHVH's divine authority. So to accept Jesus as our supreme authority is to obey all of his words and commands. And Jesus told us to keep YHVH's 'law and the Prophets' (Matthew 5:17-19). So, if we submit to Jesus' commands, instructions, and teachings, then our supreme authority is really YHVH God, since Jesus spoke YHVH's words with His authority.

If we refuse, set aside, ignore or simply won't keep some, or all, of YHVH's commands or laws, it's because some 'lesser authority' convinced us that we didn't have to – and it convinced us that YHVH doesn't care. (That's the Garden of Eden deceptions all over again). If we accept the words of that some 'lesser authority' and then dismiss some or all, of YHVH's laws we have dishonored YHVH by placing that 'lesser authority' over His authority. And if that's the case, then YHVH is not our supreme authority, and therefore not our true god and our worship of Him is in vain.

Mark 7:7-8 (NKJV), **"And in vain they worship Me, teaching as doctrines the commandments of men.'**
8 For laying aside the commandment of God, you hold the tradition of men—the washing of pitchers and cups, and many other such things you do." We read in Mark 7:7-8 that YHVH God would not accept the worship of the Pharisees, because they dishonored YHVH God when they had set aside some of His commandments for the keeping of their religious traditions. Because they have rejected some of YHVH God's commandments, means that they accepted some other 'lesser authority' telling them is was OK to set aside God's commandments in order to keep their religious traditions. Since they dishonored YHVH by **'laying aside'** His commandment, He was not their supreme authority, and He was not their true god, so their worship of Him was in vain.

Proverbs 28:9, **"One who turns away his ear from hearing the law, Even his prayer is an abomination."** If YHVH God will not even hear the prayers of those who dishonor Him by their turning **'away his ear from hearing the law',** He certainly will not accept their worship. What does it mean to **'turn away his ear for hearing the law'**? That is **'laying aside'** God's law, is to ignore it as though we haven't hear it. They reject God's law because they have been deceitfully told that it is obsolete or out-of-date, nailed to the cross, finished, done away with, and it's OK to ignore it. They then violate it at will and never repent because we don't consider it to be a sin. To 'lay aside' one or more of God's laws may sound like a minor violation of God's law, but in reality it is spurning His divine authority, it is defiantly looking Him in the eye and saying, 'No, I won't'. And that is evil. That makes a person into what the Scriptures refer to as a 'presumptuous sinner', the 'wicked' or one who 'practices lawlessness'.

Are there traditions in the Christian Church that cause Christians to 'lay aside' commandments of God? Yes, there are. When we place man's authority, as expressed in Church creeds, doctrines, papal bulls, traditions, church laws and religious rules, over God's word, spurning God's divine authority, dishonoring God, and then our worship is in vain. God's word must trump over any teacher, priest, pastor, or manmade rules, decrees, creeds, doctrines, bulls, traditions, etc. it not, we are **'turning away our ear for hearing the law'**

Peter and the apostles had two different authorities giving them contrary commands: the religious authority verses God's word. They had to choose which authority was to be their greater authority. Acts 5:29, **"But Peter and the other apostles answered and said: "We ought to obey God rather than men."** They honored God showing Him to be of a greater worth, and being a greater authority than the high priest. They obeyed God and rejected the commands of the high priest. That was an act of worship.

Contrary to what YHVH God commanded and contrary to what Jesus commanded, churches tell the people to worship Jesus, worship the Trinity, worship on Sunday, pray to Jesus, Mary and the saints, go to Jesus for forgiveness, reject YHVH's Sabbath day, reject Passover, reject YHVH's laws, and they say, 'just believe', and eat your Easter Sunday Ham Dinners. And since they are deceived by the 'image of the beast' they do as they are told.

Contrary to popular belief, YHVH's holy days, as defined in the Old Testament, were to be observed 'forever'. Jesus did not fulfill them because there is no way to 'fulfill' a memorial day of remembrance. There is no way to 'fulfill' the 4th of July, or any memorial day. In addition, a close reading of Jesus' words will confirm that Jesus did not turn non-kosher foods into kosher foods. Ham and foods that YHVH God called an abomination are still forbidden by YHVH God.

So, YHVH God tells us to avoid non-kosher foods and we are to observe His Holy days, but the Christian Church says, no, we can ignore Passover and the rest of YHVH holy days, and we can eat pork and other non-kosher foods. We will do Christmas and Easter instead and have our 'Easter Sunday Ham dinners'. Now, the question is; Who are you going to believe, YHVH God or the church? Obeying YHVH God, over the church or man, is an act of obedience, and an act of worship.

Peter and the apostles had two different authorities giving them contrary commands: the religious authority commanding them to do one thing, and YHVH God's word commanding them to do something else. They had to choose which authority was to be their greater authority. They honored God showing Him to be of a greater worth, and spurning the authority of man, even the high priest, when they were in conflict with YHVH's commands. That was an act of worship.

Most people will say, God or Jesus is their supreme authority, and they may consciously believe that. But in reality they have a different authority that is actually their supreme authority and that authority is 'self'. If God or Jesus was their supreme authority, they would unconditionally obey all they commanded, and worship YHVH God alone, and keep YHVH's law and the Prophets – but they don't. Christians can't because it goes against Christian Church doctrines.

For most people they would say that YHVH or Jesus was their supreme authority, but 'self' is their true god. While they do keep some, or perhaps most, of God's laws, 'self' decides which ones to keep and which ones to discard. That is placing 'self' in a greater authority than YHVH, or Jesus. Self

True Worship

than decides what is "good and evil", just as Satan told to Adam and Eve in the Garden of Eden. Matthew 16:24 (NKJV), **"Then Jesus said to His disciples, "If anyone desires to come after Me, let him deny himself, and take up his cross, and follow Me. "** Jesus tells us that if we want to be one of his, we must deny the authority of 'self' (crucify self), and accept his authority as our supreme authority.

We crucify 'self' by humbling of 'self's' authority, exalting YHVH God as our supreme authority, acknowledging that it is YHVH God who determines 'good and evil', not us, and then submitting to His divine authority. We read in Job 1:20, **"Then Job arose, tore his robe, and shaved his head; and he fell to the ground and worshiped".** He humbled himself before YHVH God and fell to the ground as an act that symbolized his humble submission.

WORSHIP REQUIRES GIVING

To know God is to love God and to love God is to obey God (1John 4:8, 1Jonh 5:2-3, John 14:15). When we come to a true knowledge of God as our creator and redeemer, learn of His nature and character and then come to an understand of; who He is, what He has done to us, what He will do for us, and the standard He will judge all people. We then have two choices, to believe it or to not believe it. If we believe it, we will respond to YHVH God with a Biblical type of love, that is a self-sacrificial giving love. As a result of that giving love, we will give God our time, energy, loyalty, trust, obedience, use our resources to do His will, etc., and that is our natural expression of YHVH God's great worth to us, so that is an act of worship.

Not all giving is an act of worship, but when the giving is done to obey and honor YHVH God, or as an act of submission His Divine authority, then it is an act of worship.

It's not an emotional love that God is requiring of us, God is all about a justice that goes beyond just being fair, God requires that we be like Him and that requires us to exhibit a love that is an unselfish type of giving love. God requires that we practice mercy, compassion, charity, selfless giving, and that's all under the banner of love. We are to love God above all things and to love our neighbor as ourselves. And that's with a 'self-sacrificial giving love'. So when we love God with that type of love, giving Him our time, energy, resources, praise, glory, honor, and thanksgiving, it is an act of worship. When we practice that type of 'self-sacrificial giving' love with our neighbors, that is, giving them what they need to live as healthy as we are, that too is an act of worship. That type of love in the Old Testament Hebrew Scriptures is 'ahav' and in the New Testament Greek is 'agape' and they are both acts of worship when we do then to honor, serve and obey YHVH God. To practice that type of 'giving' love is an act of worship because it is not an emotional love, but rather a choice that we make in our service to God.

Worship is first and foremost obedience to our supreme authority. Obedience itself is an expression of a 'giving' love. 1Samuel 15:22, **"So Samuel said: "Has YHVH as great delight in burnt offerings and sacrifices, as in obeying the voice of YHVH? Behold, to obey is better than sacrifice, and to heed than the fat of rams."** Worship isn't so much religious activity: prayer, singing, chanting, bowing down, lighting candles, praising, etc. Because you can do all of that to a god that you dishonor by not obeying it, and that would make all of our religious activity **"worship in vain"**. We can only truly worship God when we honor Him by our submitting to His divine authority, as our supreme authority and that is true worship.

Proverbs 28:9, **"One who turns away his ear from hearing the law, Even his prayer is an abomination.".**

WORSHIP IS SACRIFICE

In Genesis 22 we read that Abraham was asked to sacrifice his son Isaac. Abraham obeyed God, and thus he was willing to sacrifice his own son whom he loved greatly. Abraham was only willing to do that because he trusted YHVH God and loved Him even more than his precious son. That sacrifice, i.e., his willingness to do it, was a great sacrifice by Abraham to God and a very difficult command to obey, and therefore a great act of worship. Sacrificial giving to our supreme authority is an act of worship.

The love YHVH God calls on us to have is a giving love, or a self-sacrificing love. The true expression of love, is giving. And that's where sacrifices come in. Sacrifices are what we give away at our own expense to express our love, and (or) thanksgiving.

ANIMAL SACRIFICES

In an ancient agricultural community, a person's wealth was measured in the size of their herds. So, animal sacrifices were a way of giving to God a portion of their wealth. A sacrifice that cost us nothing is no sacrifice at all (Malachi 1:7-8), so the greater the personal cost, the greater the sacrifice. Worship is giving God our best. Animal sacrifices were a true sacrifice when they were costly to the one doing the sacrifice. It's not that God enjoys the blood of animals, but to give God our best is an act of worship, the greater the sacrificial cost to the giver, the greater the act of worship. That's the point that Jesus was making by referring to the poor widow who give her only mite – not only was that a great sacrifice for her to do that, it was a great act of worship and faith. That was a greater sacrifice by that poor widow than some billionaire giving away a hundred million dollars.

True Worship

Sacrificial giving is important, however, if we don't have love and obedience to go along with our sacrifice, whatever it is, will not please God.

1Samuel 15:22, **"But Samuel replied: "Does YHVH delight in burnt offerings and sacrifices as much as in obeying YHVH? To obey is better than sacrifice, and to heed is better than the fat of rams."** Without the love, honor, respect and fear that produces submissive obedience, a sacrifice is vain worship. It is religion without a relationship.

Animal sacrifices are not needed for atonement of sin, and we can't do bloody animal sacrifices anyway since there is no longer a temple altar to kill them on. However, since God has called on us to feed the hungry, we can please God by obeying Him and sacrificing our wealth to feed, clothe and shelter the poor and hungry, would be a pleasing sacrifice to God and an act of worship.

WORSHIP IS A LOVE RESPONSE

Can we worship a God we don't love? Can we worship a God we don't obey? Jesus, speaking YHVH words with YHVH's authority said, **'if you love me keep my commandments'** (John 14:15), and John wrote, **'this is the love of God that we keep His commandments'** (1John 5:3). YHVH God etched in stone with His own finger, **"...showing mercy to thousands, to those who love Me and keep My commandments"** (Exodus 20:6). YHVH God and Jesus both tie our love for YHVH God with obedience to His commands. YHVH God requires that we express our love for Him by keeping His commandments. And if there is intentional disobedience, there is no worship. In Exodus 20:5 YHVH said if we don't keep His commandments it's because we 'hate' Him, or don't love Him. At least that how YHVH sees it.

God ties love and obedience together because a Biblical love that God is referring to is a self-sacrificial giving love, and that's why a Biblical love will produce obedience. YHVH commands us to love Him above all else and to love our neighbor as ourselves. A Biblical type of 'giving' love produces sacrificial giving, and the greatest sacrifice we can make is of our self-will, self-love, selfishness and self-determination. With 'self' sacrificed, or humbled, we can submit to YHVH's divine authority and that of course, is an act of worship. A shortcut way of saying that we worship God when we; 'love God and keep His commandments'.

So if anyone intentionally sets aside any of YHVH laws, whether they are either deceived or rebellious, either way, they cannot truly worship YHVH God because they are dishonoring Him with their disobedience to His divine authority. So people who enjoy their Easter Sunday Ham dinners, are rejecting YHVH's Sabbath law, they are rejecting YHVH's dietary laws, they keep the

Pagan Easter instead of YHVH's Passover which He told us to observe forever and they worship Jesus, YHVH's anointed prophet, instead of YHVH our God, so their worship is in vain.

THE WIDE GATE AND THE NARROW GATE

This perhaps the great parable that Jesus told, and perhaps the most misunderstood parable. I say, 'misunderstood' because those in the Christian Church don't seem to understand, because they don't seem to get the message of it. If they did, they would accept the lawless doctrines of the Christian Church.

In the Gospel of Matthew 7:13-27 Jesus told us a most important parable. That parable serves as a warning for us, and explains why only a few people will be saved to gain eternal life. And that will help us understand about being a true worshiper. At first when you read the parable you might think that it has nothing to do with worship and it doesn't even mention worship. But, when we understand that being saved and being a true worshiper are synonymous, and then we will know that the parable is as much about true worship as it is about salvation. All saved people are true worshipers of God, and all true worshipers of God will be saved and God will redeem them at the end of time to populate His eternal kingdom.

Matthew 7:13-14 (NKJV), **"Enter by the narrow gate; for wide is the gate and broad is the way that leads to destruction, and there are many who go in by it. 14 Because narrow is the gate and difficult is the way which leads to life, and there are few who find it."**

In this parable, the 'Broad way and the Narrow way', Jesus equates our spiritual walk to walking on one of two paths. There is narrow way with just a 'few' true worshipers on it, and they will reach God's Kingdom. And then there is a Broad way, with 'many' on it, and they are headed for eternal destruction.

Our obvious question has to be; if the Broad way leads to eternal destruction, why are there so many people on it? And the most obvious answer is that they are deceived, for no one would travel on a road leading to eternal destruction if they knew that was at the end of the way.

The next question has to be; who deceived them? And that Jesus tells us in Matthew 7:15-20, there Jesus tells us that it was the, **"false prophets. They come to you in sheep's clothing"**. A false prophet is a person who claims to speak God's words, God's message or God's will, to the people while they are not. These false prophets wore 'sheep's clothing'. Who wears 'sheep's clothing'? The shepherds at Jesus' time wore sheep's clothing, and the shepherds of today are the priests and pastors.

So the next question has to be, what exactly was that deception that caused them to walk on the Broad way leading to eternal destruction?

So what is the message of the false prophets? We read in Matthew 7:22-23 that when they came to the end of the Broad way Jesus said to them, '**depart from me, you who practice lawlessness**'. Those who accepted the message of the false prophets ended up on the Broad road headed for eternal destruction because they 'practiced lawlessness'. What laws did they ignore and not keep? In this same sermon Jesus told us to keep YHVH's 'law and the Prophets', every jot and tittle until heaven and earth pass away. That is obviously that laws they didn't keep. And in violating YHVH's laws and Jesus' command they greatly dishonored YHVH and Jesus, so YHVH will not accept their worship. There worship was in vain. (as in Mark 7:7-9).

The message that deceived the people so that they would walk on the Broad way headed for eternal destruction is the same message we hear in Christian Churches today. In Christian Churches today we hear that we no longer need to YHVH's 'law and the Prophets'. Quoting Paul they tell us that YHVH's 'law and the Prophets' are 'done away with', 'nailed to the cross', Old Covenant, they work wrath, just a tutor, etc. And with that message the false prophets in the churches deceive the people and then the people become presumptuous sinners, thinking that there is no need to keep YHVH's law. And then by being lawless and unrepentant, their worship will be in vain.

And those who 'practice lawlessness' can't worship YHVH because they dishonor YHVH God. How did they dishonor God? They don't keep YHVH 'law and the Prophets' but 'laid aside' some of it, or all of it. John 9:31, **"Now we know that God does not hear sinners; but if anyone is a worshiper of God and does His will, He hears him."** An unrepentant sinner cannot be a true worshiper of God. God will not hear them nor will He accept the worship of those who dishonor Him by rejecting His commandments. (Those on the Broad way). According to Proverbs 28:9 YHVH God will not even hear the prayers of those who lay aside His laws – until they truly repent.

So, being saved is synonymous with being a true worshiper. All saved people are true worshipers of YHVH, and the condemned people are not true worshiper of YHVH, if they do worship, their worship is in vain.

Those on the broad way, we will learn, are unrepentant presumptuous sinners who "practice lawlessness" and so obviously they are not true worshipers. Those on the broad way, if they worship, they either worshiped in vain, or they worshiped some other god, and so they were not allowed into YHVH's eternal Kingdom. They are lost and will be condemned regardless of

True Worship

what religion they belonged to, or what Christian denomination they belonged to, regardless of what they believed, and regardless of what they confessed. Only those who are true worshipers on the 'narrow way' will be saved.

Jesus warning here is exclusively for Christians. Matthew 7:21-22, **"Not everyone who says to Me, 'Lord, Lord,' shall enter the kingdom of heaven, but he who does the will of My Father in heaven. 22 Many will say to Me in that day, 'Lord, Lord, have we not prophesied in Your name, cast out demons in Your name, and done many wonders in Your name?'.** Clearly those on the Broad way that were condemned for practicing lawlessness were good Christians. We know that they were Christians because they called Jesus, "Lord, Lord", and only Christians accept Jesus as lord. Also, these were good Christians, for they were very active in their religions. They did many wonders in Jesus' name, prophesied, and even cast out demons. So they weren't just Christians, they were good Christians, but yet they were condemned because they accept the church doct'ine based on Paul's epistles which said that they didn't need to keep YVHV's 'law and the Prophets', and they also to violated YHVH First Commandment by worshiping a Trinity and worshiping Jesus.

We learn in the parable, that those on be Broad way were on way because they deceived, and now their lawless behavior makes their worship unacceptable to YHVH God, so, if they worshiped, it was in vain. What was that deception, and who deceived them?

CHOOSE THIS DAY WHOM YOU WILL SERVE

FALSE PROPHETS

In Matthew 7:15:20 (NKJV) Jesus spends a good amount of ink to make sure we can identify a false prophet, that's very important. Jesus said, **"Beware of false prophets, who come to you in sheep's clothing, but inwardly they are ravenous wolves. 16 You will know them by their fruits. Do men gather grapes from thornbushes or figs from thistles? 17 Even so, every good tree bears good fruit, but a bad tree bears bad fruit. 18 A good tree cannot bear bad fruit, nor can a bad tree bear good fruit. 19 Every tree that does not bear good fruit is cut down and thrown into the fire. 20 Therefore by their fruits you will know them."** False prophets were 'sheep's clothing'. In ancient times if you saw someone in sheep's clothing you knew it was a shepherd. So, the false prophets today are the shepherds, they are the priests and the pastors in the Christian Churches.

And Jesus said you will know false prophets by their 'fruits'. 'Fruits' are what we produce, so fruits are our works, good fruits are righteous acts and

True Worship

bad fruits are unrighteous acts. According to Jesus, false prophets produce unrighteous acts. Does your pastor or priest keep YHVH's Sabbath day holy? Do they refrain from eating unclean foods? Do they worship YHVH God alone? Do they observe YHVH's Passover? And, of course, Christians cannot do these and still be considered Christians. So, all Christian priests and pastors are false prophets.

Jesus gave us many warnings about false prophets. Matthew 24:11-12, **"and many false prophets will appear and deceive many people. 12 Because of the increase of lawlessness, the love of most will grow cold"** Again, in Matthew 24 we are warned about 'false prophets' causing people to be lawless.

What was the message that the false prophets uses to get people to be lawless and to walk on the broad way? Jesus spoke YHVH's words with YHVH's authority, making him YHVH's anointed Prophet. Anyone who speaks contrary to what Jesus spoke is a false prophet. Jesus told us to keep YHVH's law and the Prophets, ever jot and tittle until heaven and earth pass away (Matthew 5:17-19), and to worship YHVH alone (Matthew 4:10). Anyone who speaks contrary to that is a false prophet. And anyone that is deceived by their message is on the Broad way, on their way to eternal destruction.

No one who truly worships YHVH as their true God would discard His laws. Those who discarded YHVH's laws were, unknowingly, worshiping someone other than YHVH by their obedience. Accepting YHVH as our one true God, our supreme authority, means that we will obey Him.

True worship requires that we totally submit to YHVH's divine authority – and truly repent when we fail. That doesn't mean that we always obey perfectly, Jesus said, **"Blessed are those who hunger and thirst for righteousness...."** Jesus said it wasn't only the righteous who are blessed, it's also those who 'hunger and thirst' for righteousness. It's not that we have to achieve perfect righteousness (i.e. perfect obedience), Jesus said it is enough to truly desire for it and strive for it and repent when we fail. The repentant publican in Luke 18 went to his house 'justified' according to Jesus. To be 'justified' is to be 'just as if you never have sinned', that's being made white as snow.

WORSHIP MUST BE IN TRUTH AND SPIRIT

John 4:24, **"God is Spirit, and those who worship Him must worship in spirit and truth."** Jesus told us **"God is Spirit"**. What is 'Spirit'? Spirit in the Greek language is translated as 'invisible force', 'wind', 'breath', 'angels', etc. To say that we are to worship God in 'spirit' is to say that our worship must be a result of inner force, inner drive, or inner feelings, which are invisible, but result in an external behavior of obeying God. What is that external 'behavior'? Our behavior is shaped by 'truth' and God's word is truth. God's word is called the **'word of truth'** (Psalm 119:43,160, Proverbs 22:21, John 17:17, etc.) that is YHVH's word – which was also spoken by Jesus. YHVH's "word of truth" is His "law and the Prophets" in the Old Testament and Jesus' words in the New Testament.

To worship in 'truth and spirit', is to have internal desire and will to submit to YHVH's words (spirit) and then obey YHVH's 'Word of Truth'. To worship YHVH is to do His will, not simply mechanically obedience. Our inner thoughts, feelings, and drive is our 'spirit'. We worship in spirit when our inner being desires to do God's will, desiring to submit to YHVH's divine authority. We worship in truth, when we actually submit to His authority in obedience. Love God and keep His commandments.

WORSHIP INCLUDES PRAISE AND THANKSGIVING

Heartfelt praise and thanksgiving for YHVH God is an acknowledgement that we believe that the good things we have received came from Him. In doing that we are confessing our faith in Him, and that He is a loving God who wants good for us. That makes our praise and thanksgiving an act of faith and obedience and it is therefore an act of worship.

The fact that YHVH said He would not share His glory, honor, praise, thanksgiving and worship (Isaiah 42:8, Exodus 20:2-3) with another is also saying that He expects it of us.

Psalm 107:31-32, **"Oh that men would praise YHVH for his goodness, and for his wonderful works to the children of men!**
32 Let them exalt him also in the congregation of the people, and praise him in the assembly of the elders."
Isaiah 66:4, **"All the earth shall worship You And sing praises to You; They shall sing praises to Your name." Selah**

In Genesis 24:25-25, and 52, the men who went to find a bride of Isaac, worshiped YHVH God by praising and thanking Him for their success. Acknowledging that YHVH God was behind their success was also an act of faith that honored YHVH God. We worship YHVH God with the praise and thanksgiving of our hearts, and that is the 'new song' that the redeemed have for YHVH (Psalm 144:9, 149:1, Isaiah 42:10, Revelation 14:3, etc.). The 'new song' is an act of worship. Each of the redeemed has a new sing which is an outpouring of our hearts, with praise, thanksgiving as we express our joyful love of YHVH for our creation (Psalm 95:6), redemption (Psalm 95:1) and all the good He does for us. That new song is sung with our hearts, rather than our mouths. Although in heaven we will be able to verbalize it.

"Jesus tells us to worship God in 'spirit and truth'. Here is example of worship without the spirit; Mark 7:6-7, **"He answered and said to them, "Well did Isaiah prophesy of you hypocrites, as it is written: 'This people honors Me with their lips, but their heart is far from Me. 7 And in vain they worship Me, teaching as doctrines the commandments of men.' For laying aside the commandment of God, you hold the tradition of men— the washing of pitchers and cups, and many other such things you do."** According to Jesus, their hearts were far from God. They were very religious and did all the religious things. But they did not have the love for God that would have motivated them to adhere to God's commands. So, their religious activities and rituals got in the way of keep all of God's laws and commandments.

And then, in Matthew 7:21-23 we an example of a group of people worshiped God in spirit, but not in truth. Matthew 7:21-23 (NKJV), **"Not everyone who says to Me, 'Lord, Lord,' shall enter the kingdom of heaven, but he who does the will of My Father in heaven. 22 Many will say to Me in that day, 'Lord, Lord, have we not prophesied in Your name, cast out demons in Your name, and done many wonders in Your name?' 23 And then I will declare to them, 'I never knew you; depart from Me, you who practice lawlessness!'"** Here is a group of people, they are Christians, and we know that because they call Jesus, **'Lord, Lord'.** These are good Christians, doing many good works, wonders, cast out demons, and prophesied in Jesus' name. They had lots of **'spirit',** but they didn't have the truth of God's word, and we know that because they **'practiced lawlessness'.** They had been deceived by false prophets (religious leaders, pastors, priests and (or) religious teachers) to discard God's law. So they were motivated by the 'spirit' but the lacked the 'word of truth' that would have led them to keep the law of God.

If we don't have a love for God (spirit), we will easily lose focus on keeping His commandments (truth). And if we are deceived into setting aside God's laws (truth) as out-of-date, Old Covenant, nailed to the cross, or obsolete, we won't keep those laws or commandments. Nor will we consider it to be a sin to violate those 'set aside' or 'obsolete' laws, and then we will never repent to receive forgiveness, making us presumptuous sinners.

YHVH God loves those who "love Him and keep His commandments" (Exodus 20:6, John 14:21-22, 24, John 15:10). YHVH God loves them because they honor and respect Him enough to submit to His divine authority. They are those who worship Him in 'truth and spirit'. And even though we love God and desire to do His will, we sometimes fail, as Peter did, and from the failure we can be restored with true repentance.

WORSHIP REQUIRES TRUE REPENTANCE

True Repentance isn't just feeling bad about our sin, confessing it and saying a prayer for forgiveness. It's much more than that. True repentance is brought about by 'godly sorrow' (2Corthians 7:10), a true conviction that we did wrong, because instead of submitting to YHVH's command, we exalted self to overrule God's command. So we must honestly humble of 'self', and commit, or recommit, to make YHVH our supreme authority. This is how Jesus put it, Then Jesus said to his disciples, **"Whoever wants to be my disciple must deny themselves and take up their cross and follow me."** The **'cross'** is to crucify **'self'** and then we follow him by submitting to his authority and thus obeying YHVH's 'law and the Prophets' and worship YHVH alone, as Jesus commanded.

Not only does worship require true repentance, but true repentance itself is an act of worship.

The core problem with mankind isn't just that we sin; the core problem is that our sin is all caused by idolatry. All sin is a direct result of idolatry. We will only sin when we have exalted a lawless authority greater than YHVH, and we submit to that lawless authority instead of YHVH's authority, and that is idolatry. That's why so much of the Old Testament speaks about and condemns the practice of idolatry and the worship of false gods. When YHVH God is our supreme authority (our true God), we will submit to His divine authority and obey His commands and laws, and thus we don't sin. Sin occurs when we listen to some lawless authority, i.e., self, and obey self instead of YHVH. That's why repenting of a sin(s) is only valid when it is accompanied by our humbling self, with a commitment to accept YHVH our highest authority and then to submit to YHVH's divine authority.

We can only worship YHVH God when He is our greatest authority, or supreme authority.

True Repentance washes our sins away, makes us white as snow, pardons us, we receive forgiveness, and we are justified before God.

Psalm 24:3-4, **"Who may ascend into the hill of YHVH? Or who may stand in His holy place? 4 He who has clean hands and a pure heart, who has not lifted up his soul to an idol, nor sworn deceitfully."** We cannot approach YHVH God in worship if we have unforgiven sins on our hands or in our hearts, and we 'lift up our souls to idols'. True repentance is needed before our worship will be accepted to YHVH God.

The Prophet Micah asked, what shall he bring as a sacrifice to God for worship?

Micah 6:6-7, **"With what shall I come before YHVH, And bow** *(worship)* **myself before the High God? Shall I come before Him with burnt offerings, With calves a year old? 7 Will YHVH be pleased with thousands of rams, Ten thousand rivers of oil? Shall I give my firstborn for my transgression, The fruit of my body for the sin of my soul?"** Micah was asking what he must do to get right with God (make atonement), on account of his sin. Then we are provided with the answer... **Micah 6:8, "He has shown you, O man, what is good; And what does YHVH require of you But to do justly, To love mercy, And to walk humbly with your God?"** The answer is **'do justly** and **love mercy'** as required in God's law, and to **'walk humbly with your God'** that is to humble the authority of self, and to submit to His divine authority in obedience to His commands. But, you ask, do we need to keep His commandments and laws, aren't we saved by grace alone?

SAVED BY GRACE ALONE?

And yes, we are saved by grace alone. However we have to ask, to whom does God give His saving grace? Another word for 'grace' is 'favor'. We give favor to those whom we love, to them we show grace by giving: patience, forgiveness, kindness, pardon, mercy, etc. And likewise, God gives His favor, or grace, to those whom He loves, to them He gives: patience, forgiveness, kindness, pardon, mercy, etc. Those receive that grace on judgment day will receive saving grace. And whom does God love with that kind of love? The Scriptures only tell us one way to get God to love us with that type of love; Exodus 20:7, John 14:21, 23-24, John 15:10, and other verses tell us that; God loves those who love Him and keeps His commandments. That type of love is not an emotional feeling, but a choice we make.

Why would God love those who love Him and keeps His commandments? Because they have the faith, love, honor, fearful respect, and humility to submit to His divine authority, and that honors God and is an act of worship. While those who will not keep His commandments, show a lack of faith in God, lack of love for God, lack of a fearful respect of God, and lack of humility as they dishonor YHVH God by spurning His divine authority. While we are not saved by our mechanically keeping of His commandments, but the redeemed do 'love God and keep His commandment'.

But, yet even those who love God and keep His commandments fail from time to time, and they too sin and need repentance.

True repentance is more than just feeling bad about our sin. True repentance comes from an inner desire to do what is right, to please God. True repentance is motivated by 'godly sorrow' (2Corinthians 7:9). However, we will never feel godly sorrow, guilt, shame, or remorse if we don't know that we are to keep YHVH's law and the Prophets as both Jesus and YHVH have commanded. The Christian Churches (the image of the beast) has deceived people into lying aside, rejecting, and (or) ignoring YHVH's laws and commandments.

We are told in Matthew 5:17-19 to keep YHVH's law and the Prophets, every jot and tittle until heaven and earth pass away. That is a simple instruction which is easy to understand. However, Paul's Epistles tell us no less than 36 times that we don't need to keep YHVH God's laws. Paul says; there nailed to the cross, Jesus died for our sins, the law is dead, we died to the law, it was only meant to be a temporary tutor, it is bondage, it is of the Old Covenant, it only works wrath and causes sin, etc. Paul tells us that the law has passed away, it has been done away with, and we are not under it anymore, and it works wrath. By definition, Paul is a false prophet, we can't obey Paul and Jesus, and so, we have to choose between them. To understand why Paul rejected the need for keeping the law and preached lawlessness, see Chapter 4 in this book.

So if we accept what Paul wrote, and set aside, ignore, and (or) reject YHVH's law and the Prophets, will become what the Bible refers to as a 'presumptuous sinners'. Presumptuous sinners presume they don't need to keep God's law, they presume the law is obsolete and done away with, they presume God doesn't care if we violate it, they presume there will be no eternal consequences, and they presume there is no need to repent. So they violate those 'obsolete' laws at will, and don't even consider that violation to be sin, so they never experience godly sorrow, and they never feel remorse or the need to repent – so they are never forgiven.

Hebrews 10:26-27, **"For if we sin willfully after we have received the knowledge of the truth, there no longer remains a sacrifice for sins, but a certain fearful expectation of judgment, and fiery indignation which will devour the adversaries."** If we know God's law and we willfully sin by violating it anyway, there is no atonement possible, only a fiery judgment. When people are deceived into setting aside YHVH's laws as though they are obsolete, they sin willfully. They are presumptuous sinners. Numbers 15:27-29 tells us that there is atonement possible for those who stumble into sin and repent, but in agreement with Hebrews 10:26-27, Numbers 15:30-31 tell us that there is no atonement possible for those who sin presumptuously.

True repentance requires that we feel godly sorrow, and strive to forsake that sin, and then commit, or recommit, ourselves to submit YHVH's divine authority as we humble the authority of self. And only true repentance will restore a sinner back to God's grace. In Jesus' story about the Publican and the Pharisee (Luke 18), the Publican humbly repented and said, **'God be merciful to me, a sinner'**. Jesus said the Publican when home justified before God. To be justified before God is to be, 'just as if me had never sinned'.

True worship requires that we 'love God and keeps His commandments'. A presumptuous sinner will not keep God's commandments, generally because they have been deceived into the setting aside of YHVH's laws and (or) commandments. They may claim that the love God, but that's not the type of love that God wants.

WORSHIP REQUIRES THE WE LOVE GOD

There are multiple types of love in the Old Testament and in the New Testament. However, all types could be boiled down into two specific types: emotional love (feeling), and a giving love (action).

The type of love that God requires from us is not an emotional love of good feeling, hugs and kisses. God has no use for that type of love, and never requires it. The love God wants from us is a 'self-sacrificial giving love'. That "giving" love in the Old Testament Hebrew is called 'ahav' and it literally means 'I give'. The equivalent love in the New Testament Greek language is 'agape', which is also a 'giving love' or a 'self-sacrificial love'. 'Giving' is the essence of true love. Love of self, or selfishness takes, but true love gives. That 'giving love' is not an emotional feeling, but rather an obedient choice.

So what is it that we need to give (or sacrifice) to God to demonstrate our love for God? We must give God a portion of our time, wealth, energy, as well as our devotion, allegiance, obedience, and our wills. Doing that is 'loving God and keeping His commandments', and for that we must sacrifice self (humble self) and selfishness, which, according to Romans 12:1 is our 'reasonable service', and that is true worship.

Those in the Old Testament knew that love was giving something costly, that's where the animal sacrifices were used. And God still wants our sacrifices; however, animal sacrifices are far less desirable to God than the sacrifices of our hearts and lips. Hebrews 13:15, **"Therefore by Him let us continually offer the sacrifice of praise to God, that is, the fruit of our lips, giving thanks to His name."** Mark 12:33, **"And to love Him with all the heart, with all the understanding, with all the soul, and with all the strength, and to love one's neighbor as oneself, is more than all the whole burnt offerings and sacrifices."** Psalm 51:17, **"The sacrifices of God are a broken spirit, a broken and a contrite heart— These, O God, You will not despise."**

Sacrifices, when done as an act of love to please our God, are an act of worship to our God.

WORSHIP REQUIRES THAT OUR CHARACTERS GLORIFY GOD

Romans 12:1-2, **"I beseech you therefore, brethren, by the mercies of God, that you present your bodies a living sacrifice, holy, acceptable to God, which is your reasonable service** *(or worship).* **2 And do not be conformed to this world, but be transformed by the renewing of your mind, that you may prove what is that good and acceptable and perfect will of God."** The Greek word translated as **'service'** in vs.1, could also have been translated as 'worship'. Our 'reasonable worship' is that our minds are 'transformed' or 'renewed' by the 'word of truth' so that our bodies become a **"living sacrifice, holy, and acceptable to God"** glorifying Him. We glorify YHVH God when our characters reflect His character. In doing that, we are honoring and glorifying Him, and that is an act of worship. When we praise God, thank God and speak of His goodness, we are glorifying Him. We glorify God when we tell speak of His love, mercy, kindness, patience, His forgiveness, His restoration, etc.

Matthew 5:16, **"Let your light so shine before men, that they may see your good works and glorify your Father in heaven."** YHVH God is glorified by our good works and glorifying Him is an act of worship.

Conclusion

Mark 12:29, Deuteronomy 6:4, **"And you shall love the Lord your God with all your heart, with all your soul, with all your mind, and with all your strength..."** This commandment is obviously the greatest because all other commandments hang on it. If we truly love God with a 'giving love' (*agape* in the Greek and *ahav* in the Hebrew) we will be living sacrifice that worships God, and that type of love in not some fickle emotion, but rather it is a conscious choice we make. That type of giving love will also produce praise, thanksgiving, sacrifices, charity for the poor and needy, and obedience to all that God has commanded of us.

A short definition for worship could be to 'love YHVH God and keep His commandments' – that is worshiping in 'spirit and truth'. Practicing a giving love is to worship YHVH in 'spirit', and that will result in sacrifice, praise and thanksgiving. Worshiping in 'truth' is keeping His commandments, His 'Word of Truth' which includes YHVH's laws and the Prophets. Unless we worship in 'truth and spirit' our religious rituals of bowing, praying, singing, lighting candles, chanting, dancing, or listening to sermons are not true worship.

Little, if any, true worship happens in a Christian 'worship services'. And since a Christian 'worship service' focuses on Jesus, or the Trinity, instead of YHVH, it is not acceptable worship. And since Christians reject many, or most, of Jesus' commands and God's commandments, including His command to keep the Sabbath holy, to worship YHVH God alone, to observe His Passover, the

True Worship

prohibition on eating pork, etc., how could YHVH God be pleased with the worship of those who practice lawlessness?

End of Chapter

Chapter 3 – SOME MORE OBSTACLES TO TRUE WORSHIP

True worship is much more than just going to church and it is much more than doing all those religious things we do in church: sing, chant, pray, receive sacrament, baptize, praise, light candles, give offerings, listening to sermons, etc. Worship is more about what goes on in our daily lives. Worship needs to be a lifestyle of willful submission to YHVH's divine authority. A worshipful lifestyle happens when live our lives with YHVH God being our supreme authority.

THE BEAST AND THE IMAGE OF THE BEAST

The Beast, AKA the serpent beast or the dragon, are all names for Satan, and he introduced himself to mankind in the Garden of Eden (Revelation 12:9). There his goal was to get Adam and Eve to spurn YHVH God's divine authority. He did that through deception. Making them empty promises and got them to spurn YHVH's authority by making themselves their own supreme authority. And being their own supreme authority, they were their own gods, knowing 'good and evil'. Nothing has changed in the serpent beast's deceitful message, or his empty promises, they are same today as they were in the Garden of Eden. What has changed is how his deceptive message is delivered to his victims.

Today the serpent beast's deception message is given to all who sit in Christian Churches. Any pastor or priest who preaches or teaches the serpent beast's deceptive message, that we can spurn YHVH's divine authority with no eternal consequences, is a 'false prophet'. Any church organization that teaches and preaches the serpent beast's message is reflecting the 'beast' are collectively the 'image of the beast'.

What is the deceptive message that the 'image of the beast' teaches and preaches in today's churches? It's the same message that the 'serpent beast' used to indoctrinate Adam and Eve, the message is; 'we don't have to keep YHVH command, it would be better for us if we didn't, then we can be like God, and there won't be any eternal consequences for spurning YHVH's divine authority, 'for surely you will not die.' The churches take that deceptive message directly out of Paul's epistles, and they don't seem to realize how parallel that message is to the deceptive message of the serpent beast – and how contrary it is to Jesus' message.

Accepting Paul's lawless message will cause our worship to be in vain. Acts 18:13, **"This man," they charged, "is persuading the people to worship God in ways contrary to the law."**

THE BEAST WITHIN

While Adam and Eve were in the Garden of Eden they were in a perfect environment to love and worship YHVH God by their submission to His divine authority and do His will by their obedience to Him. While Adam and Eve were created as moral free agents, they initially they had no choice as to what authority (god) they'd love, honor, respect and submit to, because YHVH God was the only authority they knew. However, true worship and true love must be products of our choice. If we have no choice about who to love or worship, those actions become robotic actions, and are not really honoring the recipient.

In order for Adam and Eve to make a choice to love, serve and worship YHVH they had to have other options to choice from. So, for that reason YHVH God had to allow temptation into the Garden, so that Adam and Eve had to make a choice, as to whom they would love and worship. God knew that they may make the wrong choice, but the door was left open for them to later repent.

So, to test Adam and Eve, YHVH God allowed the 'serpent beast' to come into the Garden to tempt Adam and Eve into spurning YHVH God's divine authority and submitting to some other authority as their supreme authority (god).

So, the serpent beast (Satan) tempted them by appealing to Eve, making her empty promises, and convincing her that it would be good for her own good and be her own god, if she would spurn YHVH's divine authority and eat the forbidden fruit. And the serpent beast told her that there would be no eternal consequences, saying, "Surely you will not die". Adam and Eve did eat the forbidden fruit, and then came to the knowledge of 'good and evil'. The Serpent beast (Satan) got them to spurn YHVH's divine authority, and become their own highest authority (gods), relying on 'self' to determine 'good and evil', so in reality they chose to be their own true gods.

And that's exactly what happens today, we don't refer to ourselves as 'gods', but we fulfill that role for ourselves. We set our own authority above all other authorities, including YHVH and Jesus, so that we decide for ourselves which of YHVH's commandment or law to keep and which one to discard.

We do that when we are deceived by the 'image of the beast' (churches with their false doctrines) into rejecting YHVH's 'Old Testament' laws, we then decide for ourselves what laws and commandments to keep and which ones to ignore. In deciding that, we are then our own true gods. And that's our "internal beast" that we must overcome, and the book of the Revelation has many great and wonderful promises for those who do 'overcome'. Until we overcome self and make YHVH our supreme authority, we cannot worship YHVH in a way that He will accept.

Jesus told us how to make YHVH our supreme authority; Matthew 16:24 and Luke 9:23, **"Then He said to them all, "If anyone desires to come after Me, let him deny himself, and take up his cross daily, and follow Me."** Jesus told us to crucify 'self' daily (humbling self) and follow him. Following him means to accept and obey all of his teachings by making him our supreme authority. By making Jesus our supreme authority we are making YHVH our supreme authority, since Jesus spoke YHVH words with His authority.

Our 'internal beast' is 'self', and that is our biggest battle. James 4:10, **"Humble yourselves in the sight of YHVH, and He will lift you up**." In other words, exalt YHVH's authority above your own.

THE GREATEST DECEPTION

In Matthew 7:13-14, where Jesus tells us that many are lost and one the broad way leading to destruction, we can only conclude that they are on that way because they have been deceived. Immediately in the next verse Jesus tells us who deceived them. Matthew 7:15-20 tells us that it was the, **"false prophets. They come to you in sheep's clothing"**. A false prophet is a person who speaks who claiming them to be God's words, God's message or God's will, while they are not. These false prophets wore 'sheep's clothing'. Who wears 'sheep's clothing'? The shepherds of today are the priests and pastors. False prophets always speak through a religious organization.

Are priests and pastors teaching and preaching that which is contrary to what Jesus' spoke? Yes, their church doctrines tell them that they don't need to keep YHVH's law and the Prophets, and they don't need to worship YHVH alone. Where did the Churches get the teaching to create their false doctrines? From Paul's Epistles (see the next Chapter for more on Paul). That makes the pastors and priests false prophets, and people who are deceived by their words become presumptuous sinners and their worship is then in vain.

As Adam and Eve's love, devotion and loyalty were tested in the Garden by the temptation given by the serpent beast, we too must undergo testing. It is YHVH's way of making us choose between Him and other gods. Adam and Eve's temptation came directly from the serpent beast, and our temptation comes from the 'image of the beast', i.e., the Church, as it preaches and teaches Paul's epistles. As YHVH God allowed the serpent beast into the Garden to test Adam and Eve, so, in the same manner, YHVH God allowed Paul's epistles into the Bible, to test us.

Jesus told us to keep the 'law and the Prophets', yet Paul told us no less than 36 times that we don't need to keep YHVH's laws. And unfortunately the Christian Church gravitates to Paul's lawless message and ignores Jesus' message about keep YHVH's 'law and the Prophets'. That's why the Christian

Church became the 'image of the beast' it's preaching and teaching the same message that the 'serpent beast' shared with Adam and Eve. But, we have to ask ourselves; Who is the greater authority and whose message shall we obey, Jesus or Paul?

A person's god is whoever or whatever is their supreme authority, or their supreme authority. The commands of our supreme authority will trump the commands of any other authority when there is a conflict between their commands. We will never intentionally set aside or ignore a command of whoever we consider to be our supreme authority.

Even if YHVH is our supreme authority, we may still fail to obey Him when we are temporarily deceived, at a time of moral weakness, or overcome by temptation. In which case, we will allow some other authority (usually self) to trump over YHVH's authority. When that happens, we have effectively abandoned YHVH as our supreme authority, and made 'self' our supreme authority. If we know, or discover, that we have sinned by violating YHVH God's law, we need to repent and that requires that we humble 'self' and restore our commitment to submit to YHVH God as our supreme authority.

When we allow any 'other authority' to deceive us, or convince us that it is OK to 'lay aside', ignore, reject, spurn, or dismiss one, or more, of YHVH God's laws or commands, then we have allowed that 'other authority' to be greater authority to us than YHVH's authority. When that happens, then YHVH is no longer our supreme authority and no longer our true god, so our worship is then in vain. And Jesus is no longer our supreme authority if we reject his command to keep YHVH's 'law and the Prophets' (Matthew 5:17-19). Our new supreme authority is usually 'self', and 'self' is then our true god. We may still go to church and confess that Jesus or YHVH is our true god, but that's not really true if we are not willing to submit to all they have commanded. When 'self' decides which authority to obey, which authority to reject, which commands to keep and which commands to set aside, then 'self' is our true god and it's the deceived 'internal beast' we must overcome.

We will allow our internal beast (self) to be our supreme authority when we are deceived about our need to keep YHVH's laws and our need to submit to His divine authority. Yet, Jesus has the words that will set us free from those deceptions, and he will teach us if we allow him to be our only teacher. And that requires that we 'set aside' what Paul said, and 'set aside' church doctrines.

As Jesus commanded, we are to crucify self (our selfishness) and submit to YHVH's divine authority. That requires that we demote the authority of 'self' to be less than the authority of YHVH (or Jesus since he spoke YHVH's words).

FALSE DOCTRINES MAKE LAWLESS HYPOCRITES

So, Jesus clearly understood the flaws with the Pharisees' way of thinking and in their teachings, and so Jesus warned his disciples about them. Matthew 16:12 (NKJV), **"Then they understood that He did not tell *them* to beware of the leaven of bread, but of the doctrine of the Pharisees and Sadducees."**

What was the problem with the teachings (or doctrines) of the Pharisees? We are told that while they acted very pious, righteous and righteous, but they were actually **"lawless hypocrites"** according to Jesus (Matthew 23:28). Why did Jesus consider them to be **"lawless"**? That was because they 'laid aside' certain commandments of God to keep their traditions. Mark 7:6-8 (NKJV), **"He replied, "Isaiah was right when he prophesied about you hypocrites; as it is written: "'These people honor me with their lips, but their hearts are far from me. 7 They worship me in vain; their teachings are merely human rules.' 8 You have let go of the commands of God and are holding on to human traditions."** In this passage Jesus again called them 'hypocrites' because they claim to be religious followers of God, but, according to their doctrines they 'let go of the commandments of God' to keep their traditions and that made them 'lawless'. So, they also practiced lawlessness, and in doing that their worship was in vain. Are those in the Christian Church 'lawless hypocrites'?

Those in the Christian Church claim that Jesus is God, but they don't obey him, for they ignore Jesus' command to keep YHVH's 'law and the Prophets' (Matthew 5:17-19) and they ignore Jesus' command to worship YHVH alone (Matthew 4:10). That makes them 'lawless hypocrites', just as the Pharisees were, and therefore their worship is also in vain.

BABYLON THE RELIGIOUS SYSTEM OF FALSE WORSHIP

Who is Babylon the Great? In Revelation Chapters 2 and 3 we read letters written to seven churches. Each of the seven churches has serious problems due to corruption, compromise, worldliness, Pagan practices, human traditions, lawlessness, apostasy, etc. And each of the seven church letters is a call to overcome their moral or spiritual deficits and repent. Many people consider the last of the seven churches, the Church of Laodicea, to the final church in history. If that is true, Laodicea is today's Christian Church, a church that YHVH God wants to vomit out of mouth just as YHVH God vomited Israel out of their ancient land because they practiced lawlessness.

Then in Revelation Chapter 6 we read a compressed history of the Christian Church illustrated in four horses. The first horse was a white horse, representing purity; the earliest Church was pure under the Apostles' leadership in following the teachings of Jesus. Then that horse turned red like blood, as the Church went under a great persecution. Then that Church was seen as a black horse, it was black because it turned away from the light of

God's word. That was the dark ages of the Church when the preeminence of God's word was lost and replaced by church doctrines, creeds, pagan practices, papal decrees and traditions. Then we see that horse turn pale. Pale is the color of death, the church physically continues to exist, and even grows, but it is spiritually dead. A dead church will grow because it makes no moral constraints on the people, no convictions of sin, and no true repentance called for. It's more like a social club worshiping a false god and the promising salvation for being a member.

The Church grew and continues to grow because people have a desire for salvation, which they believe the church can help them with. But instead of being taught the 'word of truth' they are deceived by Church doctrines. The church has become the 'image of the beast'. The people seeking salvation are deceived when the 'Church professions' (false prophets) who indoctrinate them with Church doctrines and creeds – teaching lawlessness and the doctrine of the Trinity. And sure, they also teach the Bible, but only as it is understood through the lenses of their false doctrines.

After we read about the spiritual death of the Christian Church (Revelation Chapters 2-6), it is no longer referred to as 'the church' in the Book of the Revelation. Beginning in Revelation 14, the Church, as a whole, is only referred to as Babylon the Great. Calling it "Babylon the Great" distinguishes it from the ancient city-state of "Babylon". Just before that, in the middle of Revelation chapter 13 we first read about the 'image of the beast'. That is the ecclesiastical part of the church that teaches false doctrines. It's called the 'image of the beast' because it preaches and teaches the doctrines of the 'beast' – just as the 'serpent beast' did in the Garden of Eden. What are the teachings of the 'beast' and the 'image of the beast'? All that is contrary to what Jesus spoke and what YHVH spoke are teachings of the 'beast', i.e., the rejection of YHVH' laws (spurning His divine authority) and worshiping the Trinity (or Jesus).

God's ancient people, the Jews, we held captive in the ancient city-state of Babylon. When King Cyrus, who was called 'God's messiah', came to power he allowed the Jews to return to their homeland, Israel. Many left Babylon to establish God's kingdom on earth (Israel). However, many stayed in Babylon where pagan gods were worshiped. The Christian Church today is symbolic of Babylon with their false worship, and now before the destruction of Babylon, God is calling His people out of Babylon and into His kingdom. How does a person spiritually leave Babylon and become one of YHVH's people? Anyone who wants to be one of God's redeemed people must adhere to the Everlasting Gospel. (see below)

Revelation 14

Revelation Chapter 14 is a key chapter in the Bible, because it tells us who is saved (or redeemed) and who is not save (not redeemable). It also tells us why those who are redeemed are saved, and then it tells us what those who are not redeemed must do to be saved.

Revelation 14 begins by telling us that all of the redeemed, they are symbolically called the "144,000", all have God's name (YHVH) written on (or in) their foreheads (vs. 1). That name, YHVH, is on all who will ever be "redeemed from among men" (vs.4), and that's because He is their God, and that's whom they worship. Those who weren't redeemed were not redeemed because they were "**defiled by women**" (vs. 4). Who were the women? In the Book of the Revelation we read about the great harlot (the Roman Catholic Church) and her many harlot daughters (the Protestant Churches), they are the 'women' and they represent all of Christianity. How do they defile people? When people accept their church teachings, doctrines, creeds, dictates, papal bulls, etc., which is taught in place of the 'Word of Truth', they fall into error. They error in their understanding of their need to keep YHVH's "Old Testament" laws and the Prophets, and they error in their understanding the God is one.

The doctrine of salvation by grace apart from the law is considered by those in the Church as a license to reject of God's laws without repentance and that makes them 'defiled', even though they are convinced that they are saved by Jesus. And the Doctrine of the Trinity gives them the wrong nature, character and identity of the true God (YHVH) causing people to worship the 'golden calf' (the Trinity). So, naturally their worship is false and in vain, and thus they are not fit for the kingdom of God.

However, Revelation 14:4 also tells us that those who will be redeemed have rejected the doctrines of the 'women' so they instead follow the Lamb (Jesus' teachings). Jesus (the Lamb) taught that we are to keep YHVH's Old Testament "law and the Prophets" (Matthew 5:17-19) and we are to worship YHVH alone (Matthew 4:10). Those commands are contrary to the teachings (doctrines) of the 'women' (the Christian Church) who tell us that we are to worship Jesus and the Trinity, and we don't need to keep any of YHVH Old Testament laws – and as the 'serpent beast' told Eve, 'and surely you will not die'. The 'image of the beast' assures us that we don't need to keep God's commandments and laws to be save.

Then, in the middle of Chapter 14 God gives us the Everlasting Gospel and it reads; "**Fear God and give glory to Him, for the hour of His judgment has come; and worship Him who made heaven and earth, the sea and springs of water.**" And if we look at who it was the "made heaven and earth, the sea and springs of water" we find in Exodus 20:11, within the Forth Commandments, that it was YHVH God. So correctly the Everlasting Gospel reads, "**Fear YHVH God and give glory to YHVH God, and worship YHVH**

God..." All who are redeemed, or will ever be redeemed, abide in the Everlasting Gospel. However, in order to keep the Everlasting Gospel, Christians must forsake the Christian Church doctrines which are contrary to the Everlasting Gospel and let Jesus be their only teacher and keep his commands.

Of the three commands in the Everlasting Gospel, **Fear YHVH God and give glory to YHVH God, ... and worship YHVH God...**" Worship YHVH is listed last because we can't worship God until we fear Him and live a life that glorifies Him.

Revelation 14 then warns us to get out of Babylon the Great for it has fallen, and warns us about worshiping the 'beast' or the 'image of the beast'. Worshiping the Beast or the 'image of the beast' is to 'submit to the beast's authority by accepting and doing that which is contrary to the words of Jesus and YHVH. We are to submit to YHVH God's divine authority about all others – if not we are 'worship the beast' or the 'image of the beast' by our obedience to them. And those who 'worship the beast' or the 'image of the beast' are Christians and attend Christian churches and do it unwittingly, not aware that's what they are doing.

END-TIME JUDGMENT

End time judgment is primarily about judging idolatry; all sin is a result of idolatry. Even the Book of the Revelation is a book on worship. Those judged and condemned in that Book are condemned because they worshiped the Beast instead of YHVH God.

And perhaps a natural question is; who would ever worship the Beast? The obvious answer is, no one would, except for a few Satanists, only they would ever bow or kneel before the beast, light candles to the beast, pray to the beast, sing or praise the beast, or sacrifice to the beast. But, while that is the most obvious answer, it's not the only answer. Who then according to the Bible 'worships the beast'? According to what we read in the Book of the Revelation, everyone that doesn't worship YHVH God alone, worships the beast. And that's because obeying the teachings of the beast or the image of the beast above YHVH God's authority is an act of worship.

YHVH God, and His prophets, including Jesus, all gave us YHVH's laws and commands to keep, including worshiping YHVH alone. Any message that is contrary to YHVH God's message is a product of the 'beast'. The Beast is behind the spurning of YHVH's authority, and once we spurn YHVH's divine authority, we will exalt some other authority above YHVH's divine authority. We always have a supreme authority, and if it is not YHVH, then it is usually 'self'. That's the inner beast we must battle daily.

Why do people worship the beast? Because they are deceived, Revelation 12:9, 13:3, **"So the great dragon was cast out, that serpent of old, called the Devil and Satan, who deceives the whole world; he was cast to the earth, and his angels were cast out with him... ... And all the world marveled and followed the beast."** Just as the 'serpent beast' deceived Eve into spurning YHVH's divine authority, and to follow his teachings, the same teachings are being taught in Churches today. Churches (the image of the beast) tell us that we can ignore YHVH's Old Testament laws, and worship a Trinity. And "all the world followed the beast" by accepting and believing his message.

Worship could be defined as submitting to our supreme authority. So to accept YHVH as our supreme authority and then our submission His authority is an act of worship.   In the same manner, submitting to our supreme authority, if it is not YHVH, it is the 'beast'. Because the 'beast' (Satan) is behind the deception causing us to have a supreme authority other than YHVH, and for most people, that supreme authority is 'self'. And we can only battle that 'beast' within when we are free from the deceptions that caused us to submit to that beast. Within Jesus' words we find the truth that will set us free – that's why he is to be our only teacher. Set Paul's words aside and follow Jesus, the Lamb.

The 'beast' we need to battle is 'self' and we do that by 'following the Lamb'. We 'follow the Lamb' by allowing Jesus to be our only teacher and then keeping his words of truth. In the Garden of Eden when the Serpent beast deceived Eve and got Adam and Eve to spurn God's divine authority and to make their own 'self' their supreme authority.

We need to remember that all authorities express their authority in their rules, laws and commands. So, when we are told, as Adam and Eve were, that God's laws are out-of-date, obsolete, no longer binding, or nailed to the cross, if we believe it, we will set aside YHVH's divine authority (His laws) as no longer valid and trust our own authority instead. Our own authority, 'self' then tells us what commandments to keep and which ones to discard. Self becomes our supreme authority, and our true god. 'Self' is the beast we worship. 'Self' is a beast that all of God's people battle daily. In Luke 9:23 (NKJV), **"Then He said to them all, "If anyone desires to come after Me, let him deny himself, and take up his cross daily, and follow Me."**   Jesus tells us to crucify 'self' daily and allow him to be our supreme authority. We crucify the beast when we 'follow Jesus'. Set Paul's words aside, and follow Jesus.

Satan, the devil, is the beast of the Book of the Revelation, but the beast deceives people into setting aside YHVH's divine authority and to rely on the authority of 'self'. When we do that we are, obeying, or worshiping the beast.

So, all of those who are worshiping a god other than YHVH God, are in effect worshiping the beast by their obedience to his deceptive lies.

True Worship

EZEKIEL 8 - THERE IS NO TRINITY

The core problem with mankind isn't just that we sin, it's the cause for that sin, and that is idolatry. We only sin when we have an authority that we have exalted to greater than YHVH God, and then submit to that authority instead of YHVH – that is practicing idolatry. That's why so much of the Old Testament speaks about and condemns idolatry. Idolatry leads to all types of sins.

That's why repenting of sin(s) is only valid when it is accompanied with a commitment to make YHVH our highest authority and then to submit to YHVH's divine authority.

In Ezekiel Chapter 8 YHVH God gives four visions to the Prophet Ezekiel. YHVH God shows Ezekiel the idol worship that was going on among those who are called to be His people and even within His temple. Four times Ezekiel receives visions of the idolatry that is happening among YHVH's people and in YHVH's Temple.

The first vision is at the gates of the Holy Temple, there YHVH shows Ezekiel an "image of Jealousy" (Vs. 5-6). It's an image that provokes YHVH to jealousy (or anger). *What is the "image of Jealousy"? Scholars are not sure. But, could this possible be the Christian cross? The cross is a symbol of Jesus and people throughout the world use it to worship Jesus – instead of YHVH God.* And even though the image at the gate of the Temple made YHVH God angry (or jealous), YHVH said that He will show Ezekiel even greater abominations going on, i.e., more and worse false worship.

The second vision (Vs. 7-13) was a group of the elders were worshiping carved images, paintings, and statutes of creatures of the earth, and various idols *(This sounds like the inside of many Christian Churches where people are bowing down, lighting candles and worshiping statutes and paintings of Mary, Jesus, the cross and also praying to the saints).* Ezekiel was then warned that in the third vision they were committing an even greater abomination.

The third vision (Vs. 14) was of a group of women who were weeping for Tammuz. Who is Tammuz? Tammuz was the second person of the Babylonian Trinity of Nimrod, Tammuz and Semiramis – the son of Nimrod and Semiranis. And Jesus is the second person of the Christian Trinity. *(In the Book of the Revelation 'women' represent churches and religious organizations. And Tammuz being the second person of the Babylonian trinity seems to represents the second person of the Christian Trinity the Son, Jesus, whom the Churches are worshiping).* But, then Ezekiel is about to be shown what is described as an even greater abomination.

True Worship

In the forth vision (Vs. 15-16) Ezekiel sees a group of men who have their backs turned to the Temple of YHVH and are worshiping the Sun. The Sun god was the Babylonian Trinity of Nimrod, Tammuz and Semiramis. *(Worshiping the Sun is akin to worshiping the Christian Trinity).* The Emperor Constantine, who was well known for being a sun worshiper, in AD 324 commanded that the Christian Church to worship God as a Trinity, giving the Sun god trinity different names, the Biblical names of the Father, Son and Holy Spirit. Emperor Constantine also required that the Trinity be worshiped on Sunday, the day of the Sun. Ezekiel 8 again confirms that YHVH is the only true God, and He is angry, or jealous, of all other false worship, and the worship of the Christian Trinity is false worship.

Then in verse 17, we read that, seemingly, as a result of all of the false worship the land is full of violence. There is no doubt that our world today is full of violence today. Is the violence caused by the false worship? One third of the world today is Christian and they know about YHVH's laws given by Moses; however they are told that they don't need to keep YHVH's laws, and it's the laws of Moses that would prevent the violence, but they are ignored. A third of the world today is Muslim, and they accept the law of Moses, however they also follow their Koran and that instructs them to commit violence on non-believers. Most of the other third of the world rejects the law of Moses. So, the violence of the world today could be blamed on false worship.

The Everlasting Gospel in Revelation 14:7, ..."**Fear YHVH God, glorify YHVH God and Worship YHVH God**" was the way of salvation in Old Testament times, and it is the way of salvation in New Testament times. God does not change and His gospel message did not change throughout history.

EZEKIEL 9 – JUDGMENT FOR IDOLATERS

In Ezekiel Chapter 9 YHVH tells how He will deal with those false worshipers, and that is anyone who worships anyone other than YHVH. YHVH will first identify those who are His (Zechariah 13:8-9 below). Those who are His, are those who worship YHVH alone, and they are those who were appalled by the abominations going on, they rejected the worship of Jesus, the Trinity or any other god(s). Those who cried and signed over the abominations going on will receive a mark on their foreheads. What is that mark? Since those receiving the mark belong to YHVH God, I expect that they received the same mark on their foreheads that all redeemed people will have- and that was "YHVH" on (in) their foreheads. That name is on the foreheads of the 144,000 redeemed in Revelation 14:1 on the 144,000 who represent all of the world's redeemed. They had God's name, 'Yahoveh' or 'YHVH' written on (or in) their foreheads – identifying them as YHVH's people. After God's people are sealed with YHVH's name, then judgment will happen to those without that 'seal', and only those with that 'seal' will be spared the second death in the fiery furnace.

True Worship

Here in Zechariah, we find another end-time judgment for idolaters. And here in Zechariah 13:8-9 we see some important parallels between it, Ezekiel 8-9, and Revelation14, **"And it shall come to pass in all the land," Says YHVH, "That two-thirds in it shall be cut off and die, But one-third shall be left in it: I will bring the one-third through the fire, Will refine them as silver is refined, and test them as gold is tested. They will call on My name, And I will answer them. I will say, 'This is My people'; And each one will say, 'YHVH is my God.'"** In this passage we read that YHVH will determine who are His, by listening to whom they cry out to in their time of stress during the final plagues and judgments (the refining fire). YHVH says, He'll know who are His because they will cry out to Him for relief from their sufferings, and YHVH will then save them. Those who cry out to Jesus, the Trinity, or some other god will not be relieved of their sufferings, but they will face the full fury of the plagues and judgments leading to the second death. As it says in Joel 2:32, **'And it shall come to pass that whoever calls on the name of YHVH shall be saved....'**

YHVH alone is God and alone is to be worshiped as we read in His First Commandments (Exodus 20:2-3, **"I am YHVH your God, who brought you out of the land of Egypt, out of the house of bondage, you shall have no other gods before Me."** And Jesus reiterated that same command in Matthew 4:10, Luke 4:8, Mark 12:29, John 4:22, 17:2 and Revelation 14:7, 22:8-9. But Christians ignore Jesus' words and commands, because their churches (the image of the Beast) tell them to worship God as a trinity.

Clearly, YHVH is not Jesus, and YHVH not the Trinity, YHVH is 'Our Father', and YHVH is not part of a Trinity because He will not share His glory, praise, or worship with another. Isaiah 64:8, **"But now, O YHVH, You are our Father; ...."** Isaiah 63:16, **"... O YHVH, are our Father; Our Redeemer from Everlasting is Your name."** 1Chronicles 29:10, **"Therefore David blessed YHVH before all the assembly; and David said: "Blessed are You, YHVH God of Israel, our Father, forever and ever."** Malachi 1:6, **"A son honors his father, and a servant his master. If then I am the Father, where is My honor? ... Says the YHVH of hosts ..."** Jesus told us to worship and serve YHVH alone (Matthew 4:10), and Jesus told us to pray to 'our Father' (Matthew 6). Jesus often prayed to YHVH and referred to Him as his God and his Father.

In Zechariah 13:8-9, Ezekiel 8-9, and Revelation14, were all end-time judgments on idolatry. In all three passages anyone who worshiped anyone other the YHVH God was condemned.

THE GOLDEN CALF

In Exodus 32 we read of account where after great rescue event from Egypt, and while the people were left without a strong leader (Moses ascended up Mt. Sinai), that they began to worship YHVH in the form of a golden calf. They were worshiping the corrected God (YHVH) but in the wrong form, and that was contrary to what YHVH had commanded. At judgment time the people were then divided into two groups, those who followed YHVH and those who worship idols, and those who did not follow YHVH were put to death.

In the New Testament era, after a great rescue (by Jesus) the people were left without strong spiritual leaders, after the ascension of Jesus and the death of his Apostles, so then the people again made for themselves an image of God. Their image had three gods, including Jesus who was now their primary God and the form of their god was a Trinity. Exodus 32, Ezekiel 8-9, Revelation 14, and Zechariah 13:8-9 are each pictures of end-time judgment, where all the people are divided into one of two groups, those who followed YHVH in one group and those who followed any other god in the other group. Those in the group of people who followed any other god, including the Trinity will judged and executed.

YHVH God, our Father, is not and will not be part of a Trinity of gods. He repeatedly said that He is a jealous God and He alone is God and there are no others. To worship Jesus or a Trinity is akin to worshiping a golden calf, and the judgment will be the same. As Joshua said, **"choose for yourselves this day whom you will serve"**. Will you choose to worship and serve YHVH God, or any other god?

JESUS IS NOT YHVH, SO DON'T WORSHIP JESUS

WHO WAS JESUS?

Acts 2:22, **"Men of Israel, hear these words: Jesus of Nazareth, a man attested by God to you by miracles, wonders, and signs which God did through Him in your midst, as you yourselves also know—"** Moses wrote, **"YHVH your God will raise up for you a Prophet like me from your midst, from your brethren. Him you shall hear"** (Deuteronomy 18:15). Peter tells us that Jesus was a man (Acts 2:22), and Jesus was that Prophet like him from the midst of his brethren (Acts 3:22). If Jesus was God why did he need to be raised up by God, anointed by God, and 'attested by God' to do miracles, wonders and signs?

Was Jesus born perfect, as you might expect a God to be? Hebrews 5:8, **"though He was a Son, yet He learned obedience by the things which He**

True Worship

suffered." Seemingly he was not born as a perfect 'god man'. Matthew 19:17 (NKJV), **"So He said to him, "Why do you call Me good? No one is good but One, that is, God. But if you want to enter into life, keep the commandments."** Why did Jesus say that he wasn't 'good' and only God was 'good'? The Greek word used as 'good' means perfect and without a flaw. Jesus said, 'no, I'm not perfect, that's not me, that's YHVH God, He is God and He is perfect.' Truly this is a denial by Jesus that he is the perfect God, as he identifies the perfect God as being someone other than himself.

Just as the Prophet Samuel, (1Samuel 2:26), **"... grew in stature, and in favor both with YHVH and men."** So also Jesus, (Luke 2:52), **"... grew in wisdom and stature, and in favor with YHVH God and man."** (Jesus grew in favor with God, and at some point God selected him to be His anointed Prophet.)

And, because Jesus was human and had God's favor and God anointed him to be His anointed prophet. So, according to Deuteronomy 18:17-19, Jesus was anointed to be YHVH's anointed Prophet (Messiah or Christ) and thus, Jesus spoke YHVH's words with YHVH's authority. Peter in Acts 3:22 and Stephen in Acts 7:37 and John in Revelation 22:8-9 all agree that Jesus was that anointed prophet, as does anyone who called him, 'the Christ'. When was Jesus anointed? We read how Jesus was anointed by God in Matthew 3:16-17, Mark 1:11, and Luke 3:22. He received the spirit of God, that's the breath of God and with that breath is the word of God. From that point on, Jesus spoke YHVH's words with YHVH's authority, so we had better listen to him. This is why we must listen to him and allow him to be our only teacher, setting aside the confusing lawless double talk of Paul.

Jesus said to his disciples (Apostles), **"Let not your heart be troubled; you believe in God, believe also in Me."** (John 14:1). Obviously Jesus and God are two different beings. Jesus is a man who was anointed to be YHVH's prophet (Messiah or Christ), and he worshiped YHVH (John 4:22-23), Whom he said was his 'God and Father' (John 20:17) and he prayed to YHVH God (John 17:1-5).

It seems that following Jesus' ministry, death and resurrection, the stories about him, and who he was, grew and grew and they were embellished – as stories of a legends, heroes and great people often do. Paul, who never met Jesus, but yet he tell us that Jesus 'appeared as a man', 'being in the form of God', and he was a 'live giving spirit'. But to stop any factious talk about Jesus being a walking and talking earthly God, John tells us that Jesus was human, as does Peter. John (Jesus' cousin) spent three years with Jesus, and said we heard him, we saw him, and we touch him, in other words, he was totally human (1John 1:1). In other words, Jesus got hungry, ate, drank and went to be bathroom like any other human being. Only Paul, who never met Jesus, makes him into a God.

However, Jesus, as an anointed human prophet, spoke YHVH's words with YHVH's authority (Acts 3:22, Acts 7:37, John 12:49, 14:10) and was he was attested by God to do miracles, wonders and signs (Acts 2:22). It's no wonder some people assumed he was God, but he emphatically warned us to worship YHVH alone (Matthew 4:10), he told us that YHVH was the only true God (John 17:3) and he told us the YHVH is God and YHVH is one, not three (Mark 12:29).

DON'T WORSHIP JESUS

People somehow think they are honoring Jesus by praying to him and worshiping him as God. But just the opposite is true. When we pray to Jesus and worship him as God we are rejecting what he said, and effectively calling him a liar. For he repeatedly told us that YHVH alone is God, and YHVH alone is one, we are worship, serve and pray to YHVH alone, and Jesus told us that he himself was not God. So, to worship Jesus as God dishonors Jesus and it dishonors YHVH God, and it is an act of idolatry and no idolater will enter the Kingdom of Heaven, so "choose this day that you will serve".

Jesus told us in Matthew 4:10 to worship and serve YHVH God alone. In Revelation 22:8-9 Jesus told us to not worship him, but instead to worship YHVH God. The redeemed 'follow that Lamb', that is they obey Jesus as their only teacher, for Jesus will be our Judge and he will judge us according to how we kept his words (John 12:48-50).

End Chapter

Chapter 4 – PAUL, THE FALSE PROPHET?

When we study the New Testament Scriptures it becomes apparent that there are major differences between Jesus' words and Paul's words, i.e., Jesus' gospel and Paul's gospel. The church has worked hard at trying to reconcile their words, but they can't be reconciled. Ultimately we have to choose between following Paul or following Jesus.

Jesus told us to keep YHVH's Old Testament 'law and the Prophets', every jot and tittle until heaven and earth passes away. And Jesus also ties keeping the law of God with salvation. And Paul gives us 36 reasons why we don't need to keep YHVH's Old Testament law. Simply put, those two messages are not compatible, they are polar opposites and we mentally can't accept them both, so we all must set one aside. It's just as Jesus said, we can't serve two masters – because sooner or later we will have to choose between them. Unfortunately it's Jesus' message that gets set aside by the Churches.

The Churches don't discard all Jesus said, only what he said about keeping YHVH's law and the Prophets and worshiping YHVH alone.

If Jesus was correct, then we need to keep YHVH's law and the Prophets. However, if we follow Paul and he was wrong, we will be considered lawless by YHVH, and that dishonors YHVH, so our worship will not be accepted. Why was Paul lawless? Did he get the message from YHVH?

WHY WAS PAUL LAWLESS?

Why Are Paul's Teachings Contrary To Jesus' Teachings?

If Paul's and Jesus' messages are contrary to each other they can't both be truth. And we know Jesus speaks only truth. Jesus, according to Deuteronomy 18:18-19, Acts 3:22, 7:37, John 12:49, 14:10, spoke YHVH's words with YHVH's authority, and so anyone who speaks contrary to what Jesus spoke is also speaking contrary to the words of YHVH God.

The truth Jesus spoke was compatible with the Old Testament, which he affirmed and called on people to live by it. Paul spoke just the opposite...to understand why we need to go

Jesus told us to keep the Old Testament 'law and the Prophets', every jot and tittle until heaven and earth passes away. Yet, Paul said basically the opposite. Paul said we didn't have to keep YHVH's laws, he said the law was nailed to the cross, the law is bondage, it is done away with, it was the Old

Covenant, it was just given by angels, it was only a temporary tutor, it works wrath, causes us to sin, etc. Paul's epistles give us no less than 36 reasons why we don't need to keep God's law. Why the difference between the messages of Jesus and Paul? Keep reading and you will soon understand why there is a difference between their understandings of the way of salvation.

JESUS SAID WATCH OUT FOR THE TEACHINGS OF THE PHARISEES

Throughout the New Testament Scriptures we read that Jesus continually had confrontations with the Pharisees. Jesus had the harshest words for them, and they had harsh words for Jesus, they even called Jesus a sinner and plotted his death. And that should raise a big red flag for us about the Pharisees' beliefs, religion and theology. Jesus, according to Deuteronomy 18:18-19, Acts 3:22, 7:37, John 12:49, 14:10, spoke YHVH's words with YHVH's authority, and so anyone who speaks contrary to what Jesus spoke is also speaking contrary to the words of YHVH God.

So, Jesus clearly understood the flaws with the Pharisees' way of thinking and in their teachings, and so Jesus warned his disciples about them. Matthew 16:12 (NKJV), **"Then they understood that He did not tell *them* to beware of the leaven of bread, but of the doctrine of the Pharisees and Sadducees."**

What was the problem with the teachings (or doctrines) of the Pharisees? We are told that while they acted very pious, righteous and religious, they were actually **"lawless hypocrites"** according to Jesus (Matthew 23:28). Why did Jesus consider them to be lawless?

JESUS SAID THE PHARISEES WERE LAWLESS

Before we discuss why Jesus considered the Pharisees to be lawless we must discuss what the Scriptures mean by 'lawlessness'. Only when we understand what 'lawlessness' is can we understand why the Pharisees were considered to be lawless. Matthew 23:28 (NKJV), **"Even so you also outwardly appear righteous to men, but inside you are full of hypocrisy and lawlessness."** John 7:19 (NKJV), **"Has not Moses given you the law? Yet not one of you keeps the law. Why are you trying to kill me?"**

A 'lawless' person is not one who sins every chance they get and are completely evil. A lawless person may keep some, or even most of YHVH's laws, but in rejecting even one of His laws, that person has shown contempt for YHVH's divine authority. They have spurned YHVH's divine authority, and that greatly dishonors Him, they despise His word (Numbers 15:30-31), and that is to commit an act of rebellion (Isaiah 30:1, Daniel 9:5). In their rebellion against YHVH God's divine authority they are displaying a lack of faith in God, lack of the fear of God, a lack of reverence for God and a lack of love for God. That was the problem with the 'lawless', but 'religious' Pharisees.

When a person is deceived into rejecting, setting aside, or ignoring some, or all, of YHVH God's laws, they are actually deceived into rejecting YHVH's divine authority, because His laws are the expression of His authority. Then, after a person sets YHVH's law(s) aside as obsolete, out-of-date, or somehow no longer relevant, they will violate that law(s) without giving it a second thought, they will then feel no guilt, no godly sorrow nor remorse, and so they will not even consider it to be a sin, so they can't repent –just as it happened to Adam & Eve. That's why Adam and Eve, after being confronted by God, did not repent. And without repentance there is no forgiveness.

THE PARISEES WORSHIPED IN VAIN

The Pharisee's worship was in vain (Mark 7:7-8) because they set aside some of YHVH's commandments to keep their traditions, and they didn't feel that it was sin, so they didn't repent – making them lawless in God's eyes. For the same reason Christians don't repent from breaking Sabbath, eating pork, ignoring Passover, and worshiping the Trinity – they don't even know that they are sinning, because they have been deceived. Continual sin with no repentance is "practicing lawlessness" – even if it's the violation of just one law – but the real problem is the defying of YHVH God's divine authority. That's why James (2:10) wrote, **"For whoever shall keep the whole law, and yet stumble in one point, he is guilty of all."**

Consider this; If we kept all the civil laws perfectly, except one which we refuse to keep, we will still be arrested as a lawbreaker, even though we were otherwise a model citizen. Rejecting even one law means that we are a law breaker and we are rejecting the authority behind the law, therefore we will be arrested, just as if we had broken all of the laws.

A SMALL SECT OF THE PHARISEES WERE NOT LAWLESS

Here, below, is an interesting verse; it says some (a sect, or small group) of the Pharisees "believed" and were convinced that it was necessary to keep the Law of Moses. Acts 15:5 (NKJV), **"But some of the sect of the Pharisees who believed rose up, saying, "It is necessary to circumcise them, and to command *them* to keep the law of Moses."** So, there were some Pharisees (only a sect) who believed it was necessary to keep the Law of Moses. Apparently all the rest, or most of the Pharisees (including Paul), didn't think it was necessary to keep the 'Law of Moses', which was the same law that Jesus instructed us to keep in Matthew 5:17-19.

In Acts 21, Paul is meeting with some of the Apostles including Jesus' brother James, in Jerusalem, and Paul is accused of being lawless and teaching lawlessness. Acts 21:20-21, **"And when they heard it, they glorified YHVH. And they said to him, "You see, brother, how many myriads of Jews there are who have believed** *(in Jesus),* **and they are all zealous for the law; 21 but they have been informed about you that you teach all the Jews who are among the Gentiles to forsake Moses, saying that they ought not to circumcise their children nor to walk according to the customs."** The Apostles are telling Paul about their converts in Jerusalem who are 'zealous for the law'. And then Jesus' own brother, James, inquires about the reports that Paul is teaching his converts to forsake Moses' law.

Paul was obviously not among the sect of the Pharisees that believed that it was necessary to keep YHVH's law given by Moses. Paul argued against the idea that it was necessary to keep YHVH's law. Why did Paul and most of the Pharisees think it wasn't necessary to keep YHVH's law?

WHY WERE MOST OF THE PHARISEES LAWLESS?

The Pharisees were a group of religious Jews, who at Jesus' time, felt that salvation had nothing to do with keeping the law of God, but rather salvation was a matter of their national 'election'. Election is the idea that, because of YHVH's promises to Abraham, that all of Abraham's descendants, the entire Jewish nation of Israel, are YHVH's chosen people, and thus they will all receive YHVH's 'saving grace' simply because they were chosen, or favored by God – because of Abraham's faith. That means, according to the Pharisees, that the Jews could live in violation of the Commandments of God and still be in His future Kingdom because they were descendants of Abraham, i.e., Abraham's seed, YHVH's elected or 'chosen', or 'favored' people.

However, John the Baptizer, who was revered by Jesus as the greatest of the Prophets (Matthew 11:11) spoke YHVH's words to the Pharisees and Sadducees, he said to them (Matthew 3:8-10, Luke 3:7-9), **"Therefore bear fruits worthy of repentance, and do not think to say to yourselves, 'We have Abraham as our father.' For I say to you that God is able to rise up children to Abraham from these stones. And even now the ax is laid to the root of the trees. Therefore every tree which does not bear good fruit is cut down and thrown into the fire."** The Pharisees and Sadducees felt that they were automatically saved because they were YHVH's favored (chosen) people, because they were Abraham's decedents, and that made them the 'elect of God'. And they reasoned since they were already 'chosen' by God, it was unnecessary for them to keep the law to obtaining righteousness, or to gain YHVH's saving grace, or to even prove that they were worthy to enter YHVH's kingdom. But, John the Baptizer told them that it doesn't work that way. John said, 'it doesn't matter that they are Abraham's natural seed, because apart from your own 'righteousness' (the fruit of repentance) you will be '**cut down and thrown into the fire**'.

We know from Jesus' words, that being '**cut down and thrown into the fire**' is the punishment for those who practice lawlessness. In Matthew 13:41-42 Jesus tells us that at Judgment time, it is those who 'practiced lawlessness' that will to be gathered and cast into the furnace of fire – with no exception made for Abraham's decedents, believers in Jesus, those who said the 'sinner's prayer', pleaded the blood, or for those who were professing Christian or Jews. Fire is the destination for all those who 'practice lawlessness', because God will not have those who spurn His divine authority in His eternal kingdom.

The Pharisees were considered 'lawless' by Jesus (Matthews 23:28) because they ignored, rejected or set aside some of YHVH's laws (Mark 7:7-9), so they lacked the righteousness needed to enter the Kingdom of God (Matthew 5:20). According to Jesus (Matthew 5:17-20), keeping YHVH's Old Testament 'law and the Prophets' until heaven and earth passes away is the means of gaining the righteousness we need to enter the Kingdom of God, and the Pharisees didn't do that, so they lacked that necessary righteousness. And again, it not that anyone earns salvation by keeping God's law, but by keeping God's law they reveal their love for God, faith in God, respectful fear of God, and that honors God and is a act of worship.

Paul was among the Pharisees who believed that they were the elect of God, and keeping the commandments of God may be a source of blessings, but it does not affect their salvation.

Paul said in Romans 11:5-6, "**Even so then, at this present time there is a remnant according to the election of grace. 6 And if by grace, then *it is* no longer of works; otherwise grace is no longer grace. But if *it is* of works, it is no longer grace; otherwise work is no longer work.**" According to Paul, people were saved by 'election of grace', and keeping YHVH's law had nothing whatsoever to do with their salvation. According to Paul you can't be saved by keeping the law and you can't be lost by sinning. Romans 8:39, "**nor height nor depth, nor any other created thing, shall be able to separate us from the love of God which is in Christ Jesus our Lord.**" Romans 10:9, "**that if you confess with your mouth the Lord Jesus and believe in your heart that God has raised Him from the dead, you will be saved.**" According to Paul, we are saved by what we 'confess' and what we 'believe'. According to Paul, salvation is by 'faith' (Ephesians 2:8-9) and for Paul, faith has nothing to do with keeping God's law - faith for Paul is the mental accepting of facts – and by our 'belief' in those facts' we are grafted into YHVH's elect people, Israel.

For Paul, the law is a non-issue, according to him, a person can be saved and still be completely lawless as long as they are one of 'chosen' people. So

True Worship

according to Paul, a person could be a lawless sinner, presumptuous sinner, and still be saved – even though Jesus said that such a person will be cast into a furnace of fire.

Thus Paul was lawless, and he practiced lawlessness, and he trained his Christian converts to be lawless as he was. And, of course, Paul's New Testament letters reflect his thinking, and it's not that he approves of lawlessness, but he doesn't consider it to be a deciding factor in salvation. – And so Paul is simply teaching what the lawless Pharisees believed. That's why Jesus warned us about the teachings of the Pharisees. Matthew 16:12 (NKJV), **"Then they understood that He did not tell *them* to beware of the leaven of bread, but of the doctrine of the Pharisees and Sadducees."**

PAUL BOASTED ABOUT BEING A PHARISEE

Paul boasted about being a Pharisee. Philippians 3:5, **"circumcised the eighth day, of the stock of Israel, *of* the tribe of Benjamin, a Hebrew of the Hebrews; concerning the law, a Pharisee"**. And as a Pharisee, Paul believed that he was exempt from the need to keep YHVH's law and he figured that he would not be charged with law breaking because he was one of 'YHVH's elect'. Romans 8:33, **"Who shall bring a charge against YHVH's elect? *It is* God who justifies."** Paul felt that way because he, as Abraham's seed, was selected to be among the 'elect of God' before he did 'any good or evil' – so, doing 'good or evil' doesn't affect his being the 'elect' of God. Romans 9:11, **"for *the children* not yet being born, nor having done any good or evil, that the purpose of God according to election might stand, not of works but of Him who calls."** Abraham was 'elect' solely by YHVH's grace, i.e. favor, Romans 11:5, **"Even so then, at this present time there is a remnant according to the election of grace."** And God will never take that election away, according to Paul. Paul insisted that God promised to save 'the elect' and He cannot revoke that promise. Romans 11:29-32, **"For the gifts and the calling of God *are* irrevocable. 30 For as you were once disobedient to God, yet have now obtained mercy through their disobedience, 31 even so these also have now been disobedient, that through the mercy shown you they also may obtain mercy. 32 For God has committed them all to disobedience, that He might have mercy on all."** According to Paul, disobedience to YHVH's law doesn't disqualify you from being among the saved elect because he understood YHVH's promise to be unconditional, and therefore the promise cannot be revoked. According to Paul, it's even better if you are disobedient, because then a person must be counting on, and relying on the mercy and grace of God instead of their own works. But Jesus said, **'if you endure in the faith until the end you will be saved'**, and for Jesus true faith means that we trust God enough to do what He commanded.

Romans 11:7, **"What then? Israel has not obtained what it seeks; but the elect have obtained it, and the rest were blinded."** According to Paul, all who believe in Jesus are grafted into Israel, so they are automatically one of YHVH's elect. And if they are 'YHVH's elect', they don't have to be obedient to YHVH's law to be among the redeemed. Paul insisted that keeping YHVH's law was contrary to salvation by grace. For Paul, sin doesn't matter, if you believe in Jesus.

1Thessalonians 1:4, "**knowing, beloved brethren, your election by God.**" National election is the cornerstone of Paul's messages. Paul tells the Thessalonians that they are the 'elect of God'. That is, they are already heirs to the kingdom by their election, so they don't need to keep YHVH's law or do anything else – just believe it.

WHAT DID PAUL TEACH?

The Jews were astonished at Paul's lawless teachings. They complained against Paul saying, Acts 18:13, "**This man," they charged, "is persuading the people to worship God in ways contrary to the law.**" Paul was teaching that there was no need to keep God's laws, and that people could be lawless and still be true worshiper of God, but Peter disagreed. In 2Peter 3:14-17, Peter tells us that if we think we can be lawless and still be saved, we were confused by something Paul said, and we are doomed.

Contrary to the original 12 Apostles, Paul the Pharisee, throughout his letters, championed salvation apart from the law. It was Paul's belief that it was not necessary to keep YHVH's law to be saved, he told us the law was dead (Romans 7:4), it was just a temporary tutor (Galatians 3:24-25), it was the Old Covenant (2Corinthins 3:6-8), it was nailed to the cross (Colossians 2:14), it was given by angels (Galatians 3:19), it works wrath (Romans 4:15), Christ is the end of the law (Romans 10:4), the law is a curse (Galatians 3:13), the law is bondage (Galatians 2:4)... Paul taught a 'lawless' theology which downplayed the value of YHVH's law (i.e., His authority) and the need to keep YHVH's law. And that teaching (doctrine) was contrary to what Jesus and his Apostles taught. Jesus, John the Baptist, and his Apostles all taught that we need to keep the law of God to be one of YHVH's redeemed, to be one of His saints who are fit to enter the Kingdom of God.

John the Baptizer and Jesus taught that salvation is by righteousness, and therefore a person's election is based on their righteous character. Paul taught salvation by national election, regardless of our characters, and he would add the righteousness is important, but he would say righteousness is something we inherit because of our election, not something we earn by submitting to YHVH's authority (Romans 3:22). Paul would say that our righteous based on who we are, not what we do. Paul wrongly said righteousness has nothing to do with keeping YHVH's law – he said righteousness has to do with believing Jesus is who he said he was. No wonder Jesus warned us about the teachings of the Pharisees.

And I agree with Paul that we can't be saved by keeping the law, but what Paul fails to stress is that God will not grant saving grace to those who spurn His divine authority, thereby demonstrating a lack of faith in God and His word, a lack of love for God, and a lack of fearful respect for God. YHVH God will not want a rebellious person in His eternal kingdom apart from true repentance. So the faith to keep God's law is the channel by which we receive saving grace. God give grace to those whom He loves and He loves those who love Him and keeps His commandments (Exodus 20:6, John 14:21, 22-23).

WHY WAS THE PHARISEES' WORSHIP IN VAIN?

Mathew 15:7-9 (NKJV), **"Hypocrites! Well did Isaiah prophesy about you, saying: 8 'These people draw near to Me with their mouth, And honor Me with *their* lips, But their heart is far from Me. 9 And in vain they worship Me, Teaching *as* doctrines the commandments of men.' "** *(Also Mark 7:7-8)*

Jesus said the Pharisees worship was in vain because they were practicing lawlessness, setting aside some of the commandments of God to keep their traditions (Oral laws). And having set aside some of YHVH's laws, they violated them, and didn't even consider it to be a sin and thus never they repented. They accepted the teachings of some 'lawless' religious authority which told them that it was OK to set aside some of YHVH's commandments to keep their oral traditions instead, and then they spurned YHVH's divine authority to keep those oral traditions. Their disobedience to YHVH's commands greatly dishonored Him and made it clear that God was not their supreme authority, and therefore He is not their true god. And God will not accept worship from those who dishonor Him by spurning His divine authority as expressed in His laws. Doesn't that sounds like today's Christian Church, following Paul's teachings, religious traditions, doctrines and creeds instead of Jesus' instructions and YHVH's commands?

The Christian Church today knows YHVH's laws, but the people in the churches are taught to reject them and enjoy their Easter Sunday Ham dinners. They reject YHVH's Sabbath command and keep Sunday instead, reject YHVH's dietary laws and eat pig, and keep the Pagan fertility feast day of Easter, with its Easter eggs and Easter bunny, instead of YHVH's Passover which God commanded us to observe for all generations. And even worse, they reject the First Commandment which commands us to worship YHVH alone (Exodus 20:2-3) and then they abide by their man made Nicene Creed so they worship Jesus and the Trinity. Do they feel guilt, shame, or godly sorrow? No, and therefore they don't repent for doing these things? And they don't even consider what they do as sin because they have been deceived by the Christian Church and have unknowing joined Babylon the Great.

True Worship

Their only hope is true repentance which includes submitting to YHVH's divine authority and only then will YHVH accept their worship.

End of Chapter

CONCLUSION

Jesus said that he was to be our only teacher, and he told us to worship YHVH alone and to keep YHVH's 'law and the Prophets'. Not only will Jesus teach us all we need to know, he will judge us for how well we kept his words.

Since Jesus spoke YHVH's words with YHVH's authority, his words are YHVH's word, so his words are the gold standard. All other words by pastors, priests, teachers, as well as the New Testament writers must be compatible with Jesus' words and teachings. We can trust Jesus' words because they are YHVH's words, and we can't say the same about any other New Testament writer.

As our teacher, Jesus' words are truth (John 8:32), the truth Jesus wants to teach us will inoculate us from false teachings, or if we have been exposed to false teaching his truth will help us to unmask and overcome deceptions from other teachers.

Worship could be understood as 'worth-ship'. Worship requires that YHVH is of greatest worth to us, and is our supreme authority. And if YHVH is our supreme authority, we will submit to His divine authority – and that humble and voluntarily submission is worship. True worship requires that we 'love YHVH God and keep His commandments'. That love will move us to obedience, praising YHVH, and giving Him thanksgiving.

God shares the way of salvation in His Everlasting Gospel; **"Fear YHVH God and give glory to Him, for the hour of His judgment has come; and worship Him who made heaven and earth, the sea and springs of water."** Salvation required true worship.

How many people in the churches are fully submitted to YHVH's divine authority? If they worship on Sunday instead of YHVH's Sabbath day are they in submission to God? If they worship a Trinity, or Jesus, instead of worship YHVH God as Jesus commanded, are they in submission to Him? If they eat pork and other foods that God forbids, are they in submission to YHVH? And if they are not in submission to YHVH divine authority, by obeying all of His commands, singing, praying, bowing or kneeling is just an empty religious ritual. Their worship is false worship and it is in vain.

True worship cannot happen in a Christian Church worship service because they are: worshiping the wrong god (Trinity) and they are spurning YHVH's divine authority by rejecting His 'law and the Prophets'. In doing that they dishonor YHVH God, so He will not accept their worship. True worship happens outside the church building by those who accept YHVH their one true God, and submit to YHVH's divine authority.

In order to exalt YHVH God to the position of our supreme authority, we first must humble self. We are by nature selfish, self-centered beings, and we must humble self-will, selfishness, and self-centeredness before we can exalt YHVH God. When YHVH God is truly our supreme authority, true worship will happen.

End of Book, Don